TWAYNE'S WORLD AUTHORS SERIES

A Survey of the World's Literature

YIDDISH LITERATURE

Edward Alexander
University of Washington, Seattle
EDITOR

Mendele Mocher Seforim

TWAS 405

Mendele Mocher Seforim

MENDELE MOCHER SEFORIM

By THEODORE L. STEINBERG

State University of New York at Fredonia

TWAYNE PUBLISHERS
A DIVISION OF G. K. HALL & CO., BOSTON

Library of Congress Cataloging in Publication Data

Steinberg, Theodore L
  Mendele Mocher Seforim.

  (Twayne's world authors series ; TWAS 405 : Yiddish
literature)
  Bibliography: p. 169–71
  Includes index.
  1. Abramowitz, Shalom Jacob, 1836–1917—Criticism and
interpretation.
PJ5129.A2Z93   839'.09'33   77-23531
ISBN 0-8057-6308-2

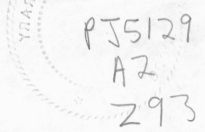

Contents

About the Author

Theodore L. Steinberg received his B.A. from Johns Hopkins University and his M.A. and Ph.D. in English literature from the University of Illinois. Since 1971 he has been a member of the English department at the State University College of New York at Fredonia, where he is now an associate professor. Professor Steinberg's major interest is in Medieval and Renaissance literature, but he has also taught courses in Jewish Studies. He is currently working on a study of the conceptions of reality in the history of literature, and on an article concerning visual perception, allegory, and audience participation in *The Faeirie Queene*.

Preface

Though he is one of the most important figures in Yiddish literature, Mendele Mocher Seforim (in English, Mendele the Book Peddler), the ostensible subject of this study, never really existed. Actually Mendele was the fictional creation of an extraordinary Yiddish and Hebrew author, Shalom Ya'akov Abramovitsh, who used Mendele as a character in a series of remarkable novels, plays, and stories that describe, analyze, satirize, and celebrate Eastern European Jewish life in the late nineteenth century. Although Abramovitsh played a central role in the development of modern Yiddish and Hebrew literature (and how many authors have written major works in two languages?), he is largely unknown today. As Charles Madison says, Abramovitsh's "stories and satire, while of classic merit and great historic interest, have become rather remote in theme and treatment. His memory is honored, but he is seldom read."[1] Proof of this statement can be found in the fact that few of his works have been translated into English and that most of those that have are out of print. Furthermore, the only way to find most of his works in Yiddish is to prowl through used bookstores or to look in the attics where Jews who no longer know Yiddish have stored their grandparents' books: as I turned the pages in my copy of *Di Klyatshe*, the brittle paper crumbled in my hands. (Because the works are so inaccessible, I have provided lengthy plot summaries at the beginning of each discussion.)

Happily, we are witnessing a renewed interest in Yiddish studies, and Abramovitsh is beginning to receive the recognition he deserves. Perhaps the most important work on Abramovitsh is Dan Miron's *A Traveler Disguised*, which analyzes the beginnings of Yiddish literature and concentrates on the complex relationship between Abramovitsh and Mendele. Although no one who works with Yiddish literature can fail to acknowledge a debt to Professor Miron, my study of Abramovitsh differs from Miron's in many significant ways. Whereas Miron is more theoretical and examines Abramovitsh's career as a paradigm of the development of Yiddish literature, I concentrate solely on Abramovitsh, offering a detailed examination of each of his major works.

Finally, I must acknowledge and thank the many people who helped me complete this work. For their professional assistance and advice, I am indebted to Professors William Neville, Robert Deming, and Rabbi Samuel Levenberg. For help in obtaining some rather hard to find materials, I am grateful to Ms. Mary Vecchio and Ms. Margaret Pabst of the Daniel Reed Library. I owe a special debt to Professors Patrick Courts, Douglas Shepard, and Edward Alexander for reading the manuscript and making many fine suggestions. For her encouragement and her love of the Yiddish language, I am indebted to my mother-in-law, Mary Kenshur. For their help in various ways, I want to thank my parents, Mr. and Mrs. Sherman Steinberg, Joseph Kenshur and, for her beautiful portrait for the frontispiece, my sister, Janet Steinberg. Finally, I would like to thank my daughter Gillian and most of all my wife Phyllis, whose role in the preparation of this book is beyond description: "She openeth her mouth with wisdom . . . and her husband praiseth her."

I sincerely hope that this work will add a little to the resurgence of interest in Abramovitsh by making him less remote, so that he may be both honored and read.

Acknowledgements

Thanks are due to the following for material:

Reprinted by permission of Schocken Books Inc. from *The Travels and Adventures of Benjamin the Third* by Mendele Mocher Seforim, translated by Moshe Spiegel. Copyright © 1949 by Schocken Books Inc.

Reprinted by permission of Schocken Books Inc. from *A Traveler Disguised* by Dan Miron. Copyright © 1973 by Schocken Books Inc.

Reprinted by permission of Ruth Wisse from *A Shtetl and Other Yiddish Novellas*.

Reprinted by permission of A. S. Barnes & Co. from *The Parasite* by Mendele Mocher Seforim, translated by Gerald Stillman, originally published by Thomas Yoseloff; from *The Nag* by Mendele Mocher Seforim, translated by Moshe Spiegel, originally published by Beechhurst Press; and from *Fishke the Lame* by Mendele Mocher Seforim, translated by Gerald Stillman, originally published by Thomas Yoseloff.

Translated and reprinted by permission of Dvir Publishing House from *Kol Kitvey Mendele Mocher Seforim*.

Chronology

c. 1836   Born in Kapulie, Lithuania.

1850   Father's death. Abramovitsh travels to study in various small towns.

1853   Lives with mother and stepfather.

1854   Leaves home and travels through the Pale of Settlement with Abraham the Lame, ending up in Kamenets-Podolski. Marries.

1856   Becomes teacher in the Kamenets-Podolski Jewish schools.

1857   Appearance of Abramovitsh's first published work, "A Letter Concerning Education," in the Hebrew newspaper *Hamagid*.

1858   Moves to Berdichev, marries Pessie Levin (having divorced first wife).

1860   Appearance of *Mishpat Shalom (The Judgment of Shalom)* a collection of articles, including some of the earliest literary criticism in Hebrew.

1862   Appearance of Abramovitsh's first fictional work, *Limdu Hetev (Learn to Do Well)*, as well as the first volume of *Toldot Hateva (Natural History)*, his adaptation of a German work on natural history.

1864   Appearance of Abramovitsh's first fiction in Yiddish, *Dos Kleyne Mentshele (The Little Man)*, as a serial in the Yiddish newspaper *Kol Mevasser*.

1865   Appearance of the first version of *Dos Vintshfingerl (The Magic Wishing Ring)*.

1866   Appearance of *Eyn Mishpat (The Fountain of Judgment)*, a second collection of articles, as well as the second volume of *Toldot Hateva*.

1868   Appearance of *Ha'avot Vehabanim (The Fathers and the Sons)*.

1869   Appearance of *Di Takse (The Tax)* and the first version of *Fishke der Krumer (Fishke the Lame)*. Leaves Berdichev and moves to Zhitomir.

1872   Appearance of the third volume of *Toldot Hateva*.

1873   Appearance of *Di Klyatshe (The Nag)*.

1878 Appearance of *Masoes Binyomin Hashlishi (The Travels and Adventures of Benjamin the Third)*, his last work until 1884.

1879– Family problems (daughter dies, son arrested for political
1881 activities), poverty.

1881 Moves to Odessa, becomes head of the Odessa Talmud Torah. Assassination of Alexander II, followed by pogroms.

1884 Appearance of *Der Priziv (The Draft)*.

1886 Appearance of Hebrew story "Beseter Ra'am" ("In the Secret Place of Thunder").

1888 Appearance of new versions of *Fishke der Krumer* and *Dos Vintshfingerl*.

1890 Appearance of "Shem Veyefet Ba'agala" ("Shem and Japhet in the Train Compartment").

1892 Appearance of "Lo Nachat be'Ya'akov" ("There is no Good in Jacob").

1894 Appearance of "Bymey Hara'ash" ("In the Days of Tumult") and "Byshiva shel Ma'alah Uvyshiva shel Mata" ("In the Heavenly and Earthly Assemblies").

1899 Appearance of *Shloyme Reb Khayim's (Shloyme, the Son of Reb Khayim)*.

1905– Spends two years in Geneva.
1907

1909 Tours Jewish communities of the Pale.

1911 Appearance of collected works in Yiddish.

1917 Dies December 8 at age of eighty-one.

CHAPTER 1

The Historical Context:
A Time to Mourn and a Time to Dance

I. *Eastern Europe*

ISAAC Bashevis Singer, in his novel *Enemies: A Love Story,* has one of his characters say: " 'In a hundred years, the ghettos will be idealized and the impression created that they were inhabited only by saints. There could be no greater lie.' "[1] The same statement could be made about the *shtetls,* the small Jewish settlements of Eastern Europe. There has, indeed, been a tendency of late to romanticize the *shtetl,* to see it as a place where happy Jewish paupers spent their time singing and dancing and being generally cute, but this picture has little to do with the historical reality. Jewish life in Eastern Europe consisted of an unending series of hardships that ended only with the destruction of that life by Hitler's forces. Out of these hardships—in fact, largely as a response to them—there developed a remarkable body of literature in the Yiddish language. The founder of that literature, and the subject of this study, Shalom Ya'akov Abramovitsh, was one of the ablest chroniclers of Eastern European Jewish life in the nineteenth century. To understand his work, however, we must begin several hundred years in the past.

No one is quite sure when the Jews first came to Poland and Russia, though their presence there can be documented from the Middle Ages. What is certain is that as the Middle Ages progressed, and the Jews were expelled from one Western country after another, they fled to the east, first to the Germanies and then after the Crusades to Eastern Europe. At first the Polish kings welcomed the Jews, who played an active part in building up the country. Under Casimir the Great in the fourteenth century, the Jews enjoyed a great deal of freedom and contributed greatly to the country's growth. Even under later kings who were not so enthusiastic

13

about them, the Jews justifiably regarded Poland as a flourishing center for Jewish life.

All this changed, however, in the seventeenth century, as the Polish Catholic clergy pushed the country further and further toward anti-Semitism. Anti-Semitism was also a powerful force among the Greek Orthodox Ukrainians, who regarded the Poles and especially the Jews as their enemies. Finally in 1648, the Ukrainian Cossack leader Bogdan Chmielnicki led his people in a revolt against the Polish state. As devastating as his attack on Poland was, his effect on the Jews was staggering: hundreds of thousands of Jews were killed, often after horrible tortures; whole communities were destroyed. And Chmielnicki was not the only one responsible, for the Poles often turned on the Jews before being wiped out themselves. Even after the uprising was quelled, anti-Semitic outrages continued, under the sponsorship of the Church and the Polish kings. Laws restricting Jewish activity were passed, and Jews were continually being accused of impossible crimes. Pogroms and ritual murder trials became constant occurrences.

The Jews understandably reacted with shock. Unable to fight back, the people tried to reestablish their lives, but they also turned increasingly to Messianic mysticism. They could only believe that the recent outrages represented the evil days that were supposed to precede the coming of the Messiah. Soon a Turkish Jew, Sabbatai Zevi, announced that he was, in fact, the Messiah, and many Jews all over the world became his followers. In Eastern Europe, where people so desperately felt the need for help, his following was particularly strong. Shopkeepers gave away their wares and people packed their bags, expecting to be wafted away to Jerusalem at any time. It was a time of great hope and fervent belief, but when the people learned that their Messiah had, at the threat of the Turkish sultan, become a Moslem, their despondency knew no bounds. Although some continued to believe in him, hoping that the conversion was simply a ruse, people generally became victims of a great despair. In addition, the learned class, the rabbis, engaged in a new kind of Talmudic discussion: not the edifying, living discussions of previous years but *pilpul*, hairsplitting arguments designed to show off their prowess. The study of the law became increasingly complex and increasingly cut off from the lives of the ordinary people. The alienation of the lower classes continued to grow, and Judaism in Eastern Europe, in the early eighteenth century, was on the way to becoming a stultified memory of what it had once been. The situation was saved by the almost simultaneous rise of two movements which, though bitterly at odds with each other, had the intention of revivifying the Jewish people.

II   *Hasidism and Haskala*

The first of these movements was a remarkable folk phenomenon called Hasidism. The founder of the movement, who is known as the Baal Shem Tov (Master of the Good Name, 1700?–1760), was a simple Jew who felt that the dry, casuistic study of the Talmud was taking the life out of Judaism and that the increasing complexity of the laws was destroying a fundamental relationship in Jewish life: that between the individual Jew and God. The rabbis seemed to be building a wall around God and allowing only themselves to pass. Refusing to accept Talmudic studies as the only way to commune with God, the Baal Shem looked to the natural world, seeing God there as well as in religious study. The Baal Shem's mystical pantheism infuriated the rabbis, for he taught that every action— eating, drinking, fasting, singing, or dancing, as well as study— could provide communion with God, could be a religious act, so long as it was performed in the proper spirit.

The Baal Shem's message infused new life into Eastern European Judaism, for he made it clear that all Jews, even the least educated, were equal before God and that they could all maintain a personal relationship with Him. Of course the religious laws must be followed, but the Baal Shem made them a source of joy. The people, oppressed by their non-Jewish neighbors and scorned by their rabbis, responded enthusiastically to the new doctrine, causing even the most downtrodden of people to discover within themselves a new dignity, a new worth.

The Baal Shem himself left no writings, but an interesting group of stories and legends grew up around him in the years following his death. These stories, many of which were collected under the title *Shivhei ha-Besht*,[2] emphasize the mystical nature of the Baal Shem and picture him as a wonderworker. After his death, the movement was carried on by a number of remarkable leaders, each of whom became the center of a kind of cult. Unfortunately, after only a few generations, the movement, while retaining its popularity, became corrupt. The leaders, who were known as *tzaddikim* (righteous ones), became increasingly concerned with their own status and wealth, and when the position of *tzaddik* became hereditary, the revolutionary period of Hasidism came to a close. The *tzaddik*, the wonderworking rabbi, became the intermediary between his people and God so that the common people, the *tzaddik*'s ordinary follow- ers, were once again cut off from God, though their proximity to the *tzaddik* prevented them from recognizing their alienation. Though there were still good, sincere *tzaddikim*, many became virtual princes, competing with each other, promising to work or claiming to have already worked miracles, and living in splendor while their followers endured poverty. Nevertheless, the movement, though now more reactionary than revolutionary, continued to flourish, for the people's faith in the *tzaddik* and in God was one of the few bright parts of their lives.

Hasidism was a movement toward the center of Judaism. It virtu- ally ignored the outside world and concentrated on inner strength, both within the individual and within the Jewish community; and it moved, surprisingly, toward a kind of Talmudic study that resem- bled its original revolutionary target. Nature was no longer impor- tant, as Hasidim of all ages spent entire days in the "House of Study," returning home only to eat (when there was food) and sleep.

The other important movement of the same period was the Has- kala, which was directed outward, toward the outside world. The founder of the Haskala, which is a Hebrew word roughly equivalent to the English "enlightenment," was the German-Jewish philosopher Moses Mendelssohn (1729–1786); and the Haskala was originally confined to Germany. Mendelssohn believed that Ger- man anti-Semitism resulted from the Jews' having cut themselves off from other people in their religious practices, their style of dress, and the language they spoke, Yiddish. Though modern linguists agree that Yiddish is a complete, self-sufficient language, this lan- guage, used by European Jews in their everyday lives since the eleventh century (Hebrew having been reserved for religious study and prayer), was long regarded as a kind of bastardized German, a way to compensate for the inability to learn proper German. Men- delssohn worked hard to help the Jews become assimilated, become more like their neighbors. He even translated the Bible into Ger- man. His program proved immensely popular in Germany, espe- cially among the young who wanted to be able to share in the general European Enlightenment. Secular studies of all sorts, but especially philosophy and literature, attracted large numbers of

Jews, and it seemed as though Jews were on the way to being accepted by their neighbors.

There were, however, two complications. The first was that while the Jews felt themselves closer to acceptance, their non-Jewish neighbors, by and large, did not. People who had all their lives been taught to dislike Jews were not going to start liking them simply because they could now quote Schiller, Lessing, and Goethe. Mendelssohn, the rational philosopher, had assumed that anti-Semitism had rational causes that could be analyzed and overcome, whereas anti-Semitism, like all prejudices, is fundamentally irrational. Consequently, anti-Jewish legislation and attitudes continued to exist. The second complication, which was perhaps more serious, was that many of Mendelssohn's followers, including his own children, having encountered the outside world through their secular studies, became so enamored of it that they actually converted to Christianity so that they could be more intimately a part of it. The unprecedented number of conversions tended, in some quarters, to discredit the Haskala; but once the doors to European civilization had been opened, they could not be shut.

Mendelssohn, of course, had not intended to destroy Judaism. He merely hoped to bring political, social, and economic equality to the Jewish community by modernizing it, by showing that Jews were also patriotic and educated Germans. His work was important and in many ways successful, but it also raised a number of problems.

These problems intensified as the Haskala moved east, for in Eastern Europe it had to deal not only with anti-Semitic governments and people, but also with the Hasidic movement. These two important movements, both of which were responses to similar stimuli, had gone in opposite directions. Hasidism was mystical, concerned only with things Jewish and inward-looking; the Haskala was rational, secular, and outward-looking. The conflict between them was so bitter that occasionally governmental authorities were required to arbitrate disputes.

As young people, especially young men, became familiar with secular learning, they often abandoned their narrow Hasidic lives, even if it meant breaking engagements or leaving wives and children. It was common for young men in yeshivas to be caught with secular works of poetry, science, or grammar hidden in their religious books. The Jewish world in Eastern Europe was thrown into turmoil as the Haskala spread. Families divided, sons were dis-

owned, and some Maskilim (proponents of the Haskala) even aided
the government in trying to break down traditional Judaism (though
many later repented of this unintentional abetment of anti-
Semitism). The conflict was frequently so acrimonious that any
sense of decency or idealism often disappeared, as each side tried to
discredit the other.

III   *The Pale of Settlement*

As the nineteenth century progressed, this inner turmoil was
accompanied by increasing persecution from the non-Jewish world.
Though the lot of Russian Jews had never been enviable—they were
forced to live only in certain border areas and were subject to
numerous special laws—and most of the Jews in Eastern Europe
lived in Poland, when Prussia, Austria, and Russia partitioned Poland (1772, 1792, 1795), most of the Polish Jews found themselves in
the Russian zone. Catherine the Great, who refused to allow Jews to
enter Russia, had suddenly annexed over a million of them. Under
Catherine and her successor, their lives were indeed bitter. They
were forced to live in the far west—an area known as the Pale of
Settlement—and were heavily taxed, though they were impoverished by laws that forbade them from holding a number of
occupations.

At first Czar Alexander I seemed on the verge of granting the
Jews some freedom, even allowing them to attend Russian schools
and universities; but with the general reaction that set in after the
Congress of Vienna, he reversed himself, and the lot of the Jews
became worse than ever. Alexander's successor, Nicholas I, however, soon made Alexander appear to be the embodiment of kindness. Nicholas was a virulent anti-Semite who would have liked to
destroy the Jews completely. Under his direction, Jewish boys were
made eligible for conscription at the age of twelve, for a period of
service of twenty-five years; and in order to further demoralize the
Jews, he made their own community governments responsible for
providing the conscripts. He also reduced the areas in which Jews
could live and imposed heavier taxes on them. It is something of a
miracle that the people survived under Nicholas' reign.

When Nicholas died in 1855, the situation seemed to change, for
his son, Alexander II, began his reign as an enlightened ruler.
Perhaps his most famous act was the liberation of the serfs, but he
also put an end to much of the anti-Jewish legislation; and Jews

suddenly began to feel that they might even be treated like human beings. As a result of Alexander's liberalism and the influence of the Haskala, Jews swarmed to the universities and began entering all sorts of professions that had earlier been denied them. Hebrew and Yiddish newspapers were founded and it was a time of great optimism. Unfortunately, this optimism was short-lived, for Alexander's liberalism waned toward the end of his reign, and his assassination in 1881 led to a resurgence of official anti-Semitism, expressing itself first in a series of pogroms and then in new, even more repressive legislation. Under Alexander III and Nicholas II, the old spirit of hatred and degradation governed Russian attitudes toward the Jews.

During most of this period, the Jews suffered horribly. In addition to attempts to destroy their religion, they suffered from an indescribable poverty, which was imposed on them by the government and often reinforced by their own community leaders. It is often difficult to understand how they survived from one day to the next. Generally, however, they managed to maintain themselves and to preserve their religion, which was characterized by a deep piety and was often the only bright spot in their lives. They also managed to develop a body of modern literature.

IV *Hebrew and Yiddish Literature*

The growth of Hebrew and Yiddish literature was a direct result of the Haskala. For centuries, Hebrew had been reserved primarily for use in religious studies and prayer, although there had occasionally been a secular work such as the anonymously translated Arthurian romance *King Artus*.[3] Hebrew poetry generally had a religious focus. As the Haskala developed, however, and became increasingly scornful toward Yiddish, Hebrew was developed into a flowery, literary medium, which was studied grammatically, and not simply for religious purposes. Finally, in 1853, the first Hebrew novel, Abraham Mapu's *Ahavat Tzion (Love of Zion)*,[4] appeared, a historical romance set in Judah in the eighth century B.C.E. Such a work was in many ways equivalent to a modern American novel written in classical Greek, and its ancient setting softened this effect only slightly. The secular nature of the book and the love theme, of course, made it anathema to the more conservative members of the Jewish community; but even a number of Maskilim were critical of it, for they regarded the novel as a decadent genre, mere storytelling, in no way useful for educating the people and, in fact, an instrument in the spread of immorality. Still, Mapu's novel was so popular that he wrote two others, another historical romance and then, more daringly, a satire set in contemporary times. Mapu's novels are melodramatic and clumsy, as they try to combine traditional Hebrew forms from the Talmud and other religious writings with the form of the French romance exemplified by the works of Eugène Sue, whose *Mysteries of Paris* appeared in Hebrew translation beginning in 1857. But Mapu's novels are also strongly didactic, attempting to show the virtues of enlightenment as opposed to the stifling effects of orthodox traditionalism. His Hebrew tends to be stilted and awkward, but this is hardly surprising when we consider that he was using the language in a new way.

Mapu was followed by a number of minor writers, but we must remember that the readership for Hebrew novels was quite small. Yiddish, on the other hand, was the everyday language for millions of Jews, though it was scorned by the intellectuals. For centuries, the only literature in Yiddish had been written for women and uneducated men, none of whom could read Hebrew. A number of Maskilim discovered, however, that if they wanted to teach the masses, to bring the Haskala to them, the logical medium would be their own language. Consequently, in the early nineteenth century a number of Yiddish authors appeared. Such writers as Israel Axenfeld and Shlomo Ettinger attempted to use Yiddish literature for didactic purposes, to demonstrate the evils and insufficiencies of contemporary Jewish life and to spur the people on to reform and enlightenment. (Many of these authors, incidentally, regarded their use of Yiddish as only a temporary necessity: once the people responded to their call, they believed, Yiddish would disappear.) One of their major tools was satire, and one of their major targets was Hasidism, which they viewed as symbolic of the superstition, fanaticism, and backwardness they wanted to eradicate. Again, many of their works are quite clumsy, both in structure and language; but these authors had no literary tradition to fall back on, no masters against whom they could compare their works. And their works were meant to be didactic, to teach, to offer moral instruction, in spite of the objections of the moralists.

V   *Shalom Ya'akov Abramovitsh*

This, in brief, was the world into which Shalom Ya'akov Abramovitsh was born,[5] probably in 1836 (though accurate records were not kept), in the Lithuanian town of Kapulie to a fairly well off family. Abramovitsh was an outstanding student in both religious and secular subjects, which his father taught him. When he was fourteen, his father died, plunging his family into poverty, and young Shalom, like other boys his age, left home to study in nearby Houses of Study. After a short visit to his newly remarried mother, he joined company with a man known as Abraham the Lame, who had promised to help the boy. Abraham, however, was simply a beggar, and he forced Abramovitsh to help him in his schemes, until Abramovitsh managed to escape from him in the Russian town of Kamenetz-Podolski. Here he came under the influence of A. B. Gottlober, a well-known Maskil and author. Eventually Abramovitsh became a teacher, moved to Berditchev, married for a second time (his short first marriage having been unsuccessful), and continued to study.

In 1857 he published his first work, or rather it was published for him. In answer to a letter from his brother, Abramovitsh wrote a short treatise on pedagogy that, through Gottlober's efforts and without Abramovitsh's knowledge, was published in the Hebrew newspaper *Hamagid*. This essentially private letter created a sensation, both because of its outstanding Hebrew style and because of its humane, modern approach to education, which recognized that students were human beings, not automatons, and that they should be treated humanely. As a result of this letter, Abramovitsh became well known among Maskilim. In 1860 he published a volume of essays, *Mishpat Shalom (The Judgment of Shalom)*, which contained some of the earliest literary criticism in Hebrew. Among the most important aspects of this volume is his argument in favor of the novel as a legitimate weapon in the struggle for enlightenment. At the same time, he was working on *Toldot Hateva (Natural History)*, a Hebrew adaptation of a German work on, of all things, natural history.

At this time Abramovitsh was far from wealthy, and his economic problems were complicated by the current methods of publication: an author would have to pay to have his works printed and would then have to sell those works himself, hoping to make a profit. It was obviously a risky business. Nevertheless, in 1862 Abramovitsh began his literary career with the publication of the first part of *Limdu Hetev (Learn to Do Well)*. By the end of that career he would be known as the Grandfather of Hebrew literature and the Grandfather of Yiddish literature.

CHAPTER 2

Ha'avot Vehabanim:
A Time for War and a Time for Peace

L imdu Hetev is a title that comes, fittingly, from the first chapter of Isaiah, for the book purports to describe the evil conditions in which Jews lived and the eventual comfort that Haskala would bring to the Jewish world. It is not a very effective work, combining Haskala idealism with the melodramatic intrigue of Eugène Sue, but as Dan Miron points out, it contains many of the elements that were to appear in Abramovitsh's later works.[1] The novel grew out of Abramovitsh's interest in the function of the novel as an instrument in furthering the Haskala and his belief that "literature is a teacher of the community" that should instruct the reader both about himself and the external world.[2] After the first part of *Limdu Hetev* appeared, however, Abramovitsh could not afford to print the second part, and by the time he could afford to, some important changes had taken place.

The most important was that in 1864 Abramovitsh had begun to publish his first Yiddish novel, *Dos Kleyne Mentshele*, which, as we shall see in the next chapter, took a very different approach to Jewish problems. As a result, the young author recognized many of the defects of his earlier work and therefore revised it completely, publishing the new work, his first *complete* Hebrew novel, in 1868 under the title *Ha'avot Vehabanim (The Fathers and the Sons)*. Thus, although *Ha'avot Vehabanim* is not his first novel chronologically, it represents his ideological starting point.

Though quite different from *Limdu Hetev*, *Ha'avot Vehabanim* is an excessively idealistic novel and is still too much in the tradition of Sue. It is, in some respects, a kind of French novel written in Hebrew, not, as Abramovitsh would soon realize, a truly Jewish work. In addition, in spite of the less didactic title, it is full of Haskala propaganda. Nevertheless, it is a most interesting work. As the new title indicates, it was to some extent influenced by

22

Turgenev's *Fathers and Sons*, though the conflict between the generations is of a very different nature. The story concerns the family of a wealthy, fanatical Hasid named Ephraim Karmoli. Ephraim is not a full-fledged villain, but he does try to rule the lives of his wife Sarah and his children Shimon and Rachel. Of course, males were traditionally the rulers in their homes, and Sarah, who is obsessed with housework, is, in general, properly submissive; but Shimon and Rachel, who have come under the influence of Ben-David and Reb Jonathan, two Maskilim, refuse to accept their father's authority. Shimon expresses his independence by craftily ending his engagement to the girl his father has picked. Rachel, however, who loves Ben-David, realizes that such independence is infinitely more difficult for a female to achieve and is quite unhappy, especially when her parents make it impossible for her to see Ben-David, who also loves her.

Shimon, meanwhile, has left town after a violent argument with his father. Ephraim is terribly upset that his son has been reading secular literature. The weakness of his position is obvious when he cannot give Sarah any reasons for his opposition, though he assures her that the boy will return as soon as his money runs out. As time passes and he does not return, both parents become increasingly worried, and Sarah consults a fortuneteller for advice. In a parallel move (and in a clearly satiric attack on Hasidism), Ephraim decides to consult his *tzaddik*, the Rabbi of Kaziv (Deceit), for advice. When Sarah goes to the *tzaddik* in place of Ephraim, whose hemorrhoids are bothering him, the rabbi is of no help, though he does propose a match between Rachel and one of his more backward and repulsive followers. Shortly thereafter, Ephraim and his rich friends force Ben-David to leave town.

At this perilous moment, the scene shifts from Kesalon (Foolstown, a town that appears in most of Abramovitsh's works) to Zalmonah, where we find Shimon studying the Haskala with Yitzchak, a young man who was adopted in his childhood by Ben-Aryeh. In a long picaresque chapter, Yitzchak tells his whole history, and then Ben-Aryeh tells his. Suddenly Shimon discovers that Ben-Aryeh is the uncle of his girlfriend Dinah.

Back in Kesalon, as the years pass, Ephraim finds that his employee Eliezer has been, with the help of the *tzaddik*, destroying his fortune: the rich family is without money. As Ephraim lies on his deathbed, both Ben-David and Shimon return to Kesalon. Ben-

David, who has made a fortune since leaving town, offers to open a
business with Shimon as his partner and so restore the family's good
name. Ephraim is properly grateful and repents for his past errors
(the Haskala is triumphant!), but he says that he cannot allow Rachel
to marry Ben-David because she is already engaged. Just in time a
letter arrives from the family of Rachel's intended breaking the
engagement, so that the lovers can wed. A week later Ephraim dies,
followed by Ben-Aryeh. The old generation is gone and the whole
world is there for the new generation of Maskilim to conquer.

Obviously, then, the basic conflict in the novel is that between
the generations, but this age-old struggle is compounded by the
problems of the Haskala. As Ben-David says, " 'The transgressions
of the old generation will be corrected by the coming generation' "
(13).[3] The transgressions to which he refers include a number of the
major motifs in the book: the lack of secular education and the
consequent sterility and degradation of the Jews; the miserable lot
of Jewish women; the absence of romantic love among the Jews; and
the fanatical, misplaced faith which the Maskilim detected in
Hasidism.

Ephraim, for all his fanaticism, means well, and he operates from
the traditional view that a father has complete domination over his
wife and children. Nevertheless, his fanaticism blinds him to the
weaknesses of this position. His opposition to the Haskala, for instance, has no foundation, as we see in one of the novel's funniest
sections. After Shimon has left home, Ephraim and Sarah, in a scene
reminiscent of the book burning in *Don Quixote*, go through their
son's books in an attempt to find and destroy the books that have
corrupted him. Ephraim, not feeling well, asks Sarah to go through
the books and separate the bad ones, but she refuses, saying that she
is only a simple woman and cannot possibly make such judgments.
Ephraim is shocked that she thinks it necessary to read secular
books in order to recognize them. " 'It is forbidden for a Jewish man
to read secular books and to deal with secular knowledge' " (22), he
explains; but Sarah, quite properly, asks how he knows the books
are evil if he has not read them. Ephraim is stunned, for he has no
answer, except to reprove her for asking silly questions.

Ephraim goes to explain that one can easily tell the good books
from the bad: " 'By the grace of God, there are only two Hebrew
publishing houses in the country [that is, "Thank God for Czarist
censorship!"]. The one in Vilna prints both good and bad books,

while the one in Zhitomir prints only good books, no high-flown books on the rules of *dikduk* [grammar, one of the favorite subjects of the Haskala]' " (22). When Sarah asks what this *dikduk* is that he so thoroughly condemns, he is again stunned, for he simply does not know, though he tells her that he cannot explain because such things are too hard for women to understand. In short, Ephraim acts out of total ignorance. He does not know what he is opposed to, only that it is something new and therefore worthy of his hatred, especially because such wise men as the Rabbi of Kaziv tell him that he should oppose it.

Later on, using the language of the prayer book, the narrator explains why such wise men are so bitterly opposed to the Haskala: "What would they be, what would their lives be, what would their righteousness or their strength or their greatness be if a new light were to shine upon Zion, and the victims of their vanity and foolishness would abandon them?" (33). One of the Haskala's constant charges against Hasidism was that the *tzaddikim* kept their followers in ignorance so that the poor would not be able to recognize their leaders' dishonesty, and this is the accusation that Abramovitsh is making. (Later in his career, when he abandoned anti-Hasidic satire, he transferred this same accusation to the community leaders, who also benefited from the ignorance and gullibility of their people.)

Historically, the Haskala was most often attacked for leading Jews away from their faith. That this charge was not always spurious can be seen in the example of Mendelssohn's family, as well as the thousands of apostates and converts from Judaism. Part of the propagandistic nature of *Ha'avot Vehabanim* lies in the unblemished Judaism of its Maskilim. Many Maskilim were, like Abramovitsh, religious throughout their lives, and such Maskilim were justified in holding that the Haskala was not incompatible with religion; but it was certainly naive—or deceptive—to pretend that all Maskilim were deeply religious. Thus Reb Jonathan says that blintzes, a traditional food, are good, but only when accompanied by Torah, traditional learning, and that people must learn to reconcile secular knowledge and the fear of God. Jonathan and Ben-David, "the messengers of the Haskala in Kesalon" (12), are both upright, unselfish, religious men, while their opponents are either ignorant or obvious charlatans. The novel never raises the question of whether a Maskil could be selfish, unfeeling, or even a villain. In fact, the picture of

the Haskala that Abramovitsh presents here is rather tame. It consists largely of reading secular books, of appreciating the natural
world, and of discovering romantic love—although on this last point
Jonathan and Ben-David disagree, with Jonathan saying that Ben-
David's love for Rachel is ruining him. Both of them, as well as
Ben-Aryeh and Shimon, believe that education is a panacea that will
cure all the ills that afflict Judaism. They also believe that parents
should not be allowed complete domination over their children, and
especially that parents should not pick their children's spouses.

Though these beliefs may seem reasonable, they were the basis of
innumerable conflicts. As Shimon writes to his parents: " 'What am
I to do if my heart is awake and sleep has been removed from my
eyes? What am I to do if my youthful spirit refuses to return to
sleep, if it rouses me to study and seek answers to my questions, to
the new questions which occur to me daily?' " (21). Just as he can no
longer understand his parents, they can no longer understand him.
They are so content with the old ways that they have sanctified
them, while Shimon is intent on questioning and understanding. As
we will see, Abramovitsh later modified his views on education as a
panacea, but he always believed that it was important. He also
believed in the virtue of romantic love (as can be seen in his letters
to his wife-to-be), and he was absolutely opposed to the tyrannical
power parents wielded over their children, especially their female
children.

In fact, it is no exaggeration to say that Abramovitsh was an early
feminist. Just as he was concerned about the oppressive life of Jews
in general, so he was concerned about the additional suffering of
Jewish women. He returns to this point many times in *Ha'avot
Vehabanim*. Sarah, for instance, begins as a comic figure. She is
simply obsessed by housework: practically all she ever thinks or
talks about is cleaning, cooking, and the unreliability of her servants. At first this is funny, but it gradually becomes annoying, both
to Ephraim and to the reader; and we soon realize that Sarah has
never been encouraged to think about anything else. Women were
not supposed to think or read or lead any kind of existence aside
from housework and child rearing. Sarah, a perfect product of that
kind of existence, serves as a kind of inspiration to Rachel, who vows
that she will never follow in her mother's footsteps, though that is
precisely the kind of future that her parents envision for her.
Rachel, in fact, is one of the most pathetic characters in the book, as

she sees herself condemned, in spite of her intelligence, to a life of servitude. Her intended husband, for example, in addition to being extraordinarily ugly, is a complete fool, and yet she will have to be submissive to him. No wonder she tells Shimon, " 'You are a man and can do whatever seems good to you. If you want to study, you go and study in this school or that. The whole world is before you. But I am a woman, and there is nothing before me: I must stay in my father's house while I am young and in my husband's house later. What value do I have?' " (11); and a little while later, " 'How happy you men are,' said Rachel jealously, 'Oh, if only I were a man . . .' " (18). Shimon offers her some encouragement, but when he is gone and she is not allowed to see Ben-David, she is truly alone and miserable, for her parents are incapable of understanding her. A woman in her position was not allowed any aspirations or personal choices, and her rebellion staggers them. Thus, when Ephraim learns that she will not marry the man he has chosen, he angrily exclaims, " 'So who asked her whether she wants to or not? . . . Okay. If she doesn't want to today, she will tomorrow' " (36). Only when he is on his death bed and knows that the projected match has been called off does he ask Rachel if she wants to marry Ben-David, and by that point his act is only symbolic, a sign that he understands his daughter's aspirations and that he has been liberated from the constraints of his old life.

Abramovitsh's feminism appears also in the opening paragraphs of the book's fourth chapter, which describe in some detail the hard life of an ordinary Jewish woman, the kind of life that we will examine in more detail when we consider his next novel. The hard, demeaning life of women is apparent, too, in Abramovitsh's treatment of love. Although the Bible contains some beautiful passages on love, including the whole *Song of Songs*, such passages were always viewed as allegories; and romantic love, by and large, was banished from Judaism. Marriages were arranged, and the betrothed couple might not even have met until just before the wedding. As Jonathan says: " 'Ask a Jewish man, "What is love?" and he'll tell you: "We are commanded to love the Lord and to love our neighbors as ourselves, as it is written." But that a man might love a woman, or a woman love a man, that he doesn't know. Such love he regards as a shame, a disgrace, and if you talk to them about it, the people will make you into a laughingstock' " (13). Jonathan, of course, is correct; and many Maskilim advocated the rediscovery of romantic love in Jewish life (though many did not, and regarded the presence of such love in the novels as a corrupting influence). Even Jonathan develops some doubts: "Jonathan's spirit wept secretly for Ben-David, because he saw that love was no good for him but that he was powerless to help. As Ben-David's joy grew, so grew Jonathan's sadness, and when Ben-David told him of his happiness, Jonathan regarded him with great pity as a lost man" (32).

Romantic love, of course, had already appeared in Hebrew literature, in Mapu's *Ahavat Tzion*, but that story was set twenty-five hundred years in the past. Abramovitsh, by discussing and encouraging romantic love in modern times, was on perilous ground, and even a freethinker like Jonathan is disturbed by its effects. It is interesting that, although romantic love had already appeared in Yiddish works (for example, in several of Axenfeld's works), after *Ha'avot Vehabanim* it plays only a very minor part in Abramovitsh's novels until the 1880s. This strand, which could easily have become a major theme in his writings, disappeared because Abramovitsh realized that it was basically foreign to the Jewish experience. Instead, it was replaced by another strand, which appears briefly in *Ha'avot Vehabanim* and becomes dominant in his later works: the fate of the common people. Most of the book concentrates either on Ephraim's wealthy family or on the ideals of the Maskilim, but there are a number of places where Abramovitsh focuses on the difficult lives of the common Jews.

One such chapter is entitled "And These Are the Generations of Isaac" (Genesis, 25:19). This chapter, which contains the life story of Shimon's friend Yitzchak (Isaac, in English), foreshadows *Dos Kleyne Mentshele* in its use of the picaresque and in its realistic descriptions of poverty in Jewish life. It shows Yitzchak's impoverished childhood, his apprenticeship to a dishonest wonder worker, and his rescue by Ben-Aryeh. Here, for the first time, Abramovitsh found his true element; and, in spite of some obvious exaggerations in the interest of Haskala propaganda, this is one of the most effective and realistic chapters in the novel. It is surpassed only by the chapter in which Ben-Aryeh tells his own story.

Ben-Aryeh tells Shimon how he wasted his early life until he found himself with a wife and children, beset by great poverty. Suddenly his family was struck by a series of tragedies. First his daughter died of hunger, then he had to send his son away in order to avoid the czar's cruel conscription laws. (In *Limdu Hetev*, the son had turned out to be Ben-David, but, fortunately, Abramovitsh removed this coincidence from the revised novel.) Gradually his wife went mad after losing these two children and she and her remaining children also died, leaving Ben-Aryeh alone in the world and without his old faith in Hasidism. Eventually he began to lead a life of sin (in *Limdu Hetev* he was a highwayman!) until he rescued Yitzchak and returned to a respectable way of life. Abramovitsh's description of the mother's madness is truly touching:

> "I remember when my two youngest children were on their sickbed, she went over to them as they were dying, held them in her arms, and said with a terrible laugh, with a laugh full of madness, which wounded me like an arrow in my heart, 'My children, just a little while and you will be happy, you'll forget all your sorrows and you'll rest peacefully in the lap of death. You'll no longer endure want or hunger. Go, my children. Go the way of all the earth, and I will soon come after you. I hope you won't have to wait long for me. Tell your sister I will soon come to her. Perhaps you will even see him there, your brother. . . .' When she had said this, her face shone with a fearful light that frightened body and soul, and she laid the children down on the bed, but they were already dead. . . ." (43–44)

The pathos here certainly verges on melodrama, but, as in almost all his works, Abramovitsh kept the melodrama under control. The scene is pathetic, but we know that such scenes must have occurred many times as a result of the persecutions and oppressions that beset the Jews. Abramovitsh did not invent scenes like this: he merely recorded the reality that he saw.

At the same time, he also recorded some of the beauties of Jewish life. For example, in a passage in which the narrator addresses "my poor people," he describes the everyday poverty of the common folk and contrasts it with their spiritual richness, expecially on the Sabbath and on holidays. "You are," he tells them, "both a slave and a king, a pauper and a rich man, naked and dressed in splendor, hungry and satisfied . . ." (46). Their religion, their belief and trust in God, their spirituality save them, transform them from worms to men, though as Ben-Aryeh points out, their belief in the Torah has also caused their troubles. This contradiction—that their belief has saved them at the same time that it has caused their trouble—runs through Abramovitsh's works; and he is not afraid to question and even, in Hasidic tradition, to accuse God. But here the emphasis is on the common people, on the everyday aspects of ordinary Jewish

life, its poverty and its richness, and here we have Abramovitsh at
his most effective, laying out the path he was to follow for many
years. As Miron points out, these realistic descriptions of everyday
life have a double purpose, in line with the ancient idea that literature should both delight the reader and teach him. They delight by
presenting what is familiar and they teach by showing which aspects
of life require reform.[4]

Of course, many of the early Hebrew (and Yiddish) authors shared
the "delight and teach" philosophy, but usually they taught more
than they delighted. A large part of Abramovitsh's importance lies in
the emphasis he put on delighting. This is not to say that he pan-
dered to the lowest instincts of the masses, but rather that he informed his writings with artistry to a greater extent than any of his
predecessors. Hebrew and Yiddish literature began as didactic
tools, and Abramovitsh, having no real literary tradition on which to
rely, transformed them both into artistic modes of expression
through his attention to structure, his careful use of natural description,[5] his attempts at realism, and his painstaking care with language. Thus Ben-David, in a long discussion with some of his disciples, makes some important points about Jewish literature: it must
come from the people and be accessible to them, it must reflect
Jewish life and Jewish traditions (one of the reasons that Abramovitsh soon abandoned the love story), and it must speak to the
heart and feelings of the people.

Still, even at this early stage in his career, Abramovitsh did not
simply intend to improve the people's taste. He wanted to help
them exercise their rational controls over the world in which they
lived, to be able to make educated distinctions between what was
true and what was not.[6] As always throughout his career, his sense
of artistry did not dominate his zeal for reform, but *Ha'avot Vehabanim* is one of the first works in Hebrew that attempted to strike a
balance between artistry and didacticism.

Ha'avot Vehabanim, then, is an important novel, if not a very
successful one. It is far too naive and idealistic, far too simplistic in
showing the triumph of the Haskala. In addition, it depends too
much on foreign models like the works of Sue for its basic movement. And between the time of *Limdu Hetev* and *Ha'avot Vehabanim* Abramovitsh made an important, if obvious, discovery: a
work that was intended to reach the masses was nearly useless if it
was written in a language that they did not understand. The use of

Hebrew may have had symbolic importance in terms of nationalism and the Haskala; but such symbolism defeated Abramovitsh's real purpose. Consequently, he decided to write his next work, *Dos Kleyne Mentshele*, in Yiddish, though here again he differed from his contemporaries. Instead of regarding his Yiddish work as a temporary step in bringing the people to enlightenment, he devoted the same attention to the Yiddish language that he had to Hebrew. In his subsequent works, Yiddish is not a language to be ashamed of; and in fact, he did not write another fictional work in Hebrew until 1886. Yiddish became his real medium, and it is as a Yiddish author that he is most famous.

CHAPTER 3

Dos Kleyne Mentshele:
A Time to Weep

I *The Yiddish Career*

ABRAMOVITSH'S decision to continue his novelistic career in Yiddish rather than Hebrew was of the greatest importance both for Abramovitsh himself and for the subsequent development of Yiddish literature. It marked the beginning of his career as an author whose work bore on the everyday lives of his people, and it set the course that Yiddish literature was to take for the next hundred years. This is not, however, to say that Abramovitsh singlehandedly created Yiddish literature, that like God he fashioned it from complete nothingness. Rather, part of his genius consisted of his ability to synthesize the life he knew in the *shtetl*, the traditions of Yiddish literature, and the traditions of European and Russian literature into a distinctly Jewish artistic construct.

Abramovitsh did not make his decision without a great deal of deliberation. Although still a young man, he already had a reputation as a fine Hebrew stylist and a Maskil. To devote himself to writing Yiddish would appear to be an abandonment of all that he had previously undertaken. Certainly other Maskilim had written in Yiddish, but only in order to propagandize, to turn the people toward Haskala, which usually meant, ultimately, away from Yiddish. Such writers regretted the necessity of writing in Yiddish, as we have seen, and regarded their work as only a transitory stage in the indoctrination of the whole Jewish people; consequently their work is often condescending, didactic, and of a poor quality. The few writers who took Yiddish literature at all seriously, like Axenfeld, tended not to be very highly regarded. But Abramovitsh knew that in the midnineteenth century, writing Hebrew was, because of the small number of potential readers, an almost sterile task. He wanted to reach the people, to convey to them the virtues of education, of self-realization combined with the practice of their religion; and he knew that in order to do so he would have to use the language of the people. Fortunately, he was more than a propagandist—he was also an artist, as he had already shown—and he brought his artistry and his knowledge of literary theory and practice to his Yiddish work. He wanted to make the people aware of their own social shortcomings as well as their potential and at the same time to raise their artistic acumen. As he said in his critical work *Eyn Mishpat* in 1867: "A literature that has no connection with the people and their needs and which is not affected by them, cannot affect them. It holds no interest for the people and is superfluous to their lives. The people marvel over what this literature is all about and ask, 'What is this? What kind of help does it bring? What is the writer doing?' And the writers become confused and don't know how to answer. Woe to such writers, who write without end, if they meet an ordinary person who simply asks these questions."[1] The people must be reached, and it was Abramovitsh's opinion in 1864 that he could reach them in their language without compromising his artistic standards. Of course, he continued to write in Hebrew throughout the rest of his life, but it was his Yiddish works that were loved by the people and that brought him—or his character Mendele Mocher Seforim—the greatest fame.

The publication in 1864, then, of *Dos Kleyne Mentshele (The Little Man)*[2] marks a turning point in Yiddish literature. It also marks the appearance of Abramovitsh's most important character, Mendele Mocher Seforim, the alleged editor, narrator, or author of almost all of Abramovitsh's work.[3] The story of how Mendele came into being is told by Abramovitsh in Sholem Aleichem's essay "Fir Zenen Mir Gezesn": *Dos Kleyne Mentshele* began as a short story that Abramovitsh wrote in a few days' time and that he decided to submit to the Yiddish newspaper *Kol M'vasser*, whose editor was Alexander Tzederboim. Because Yiddish was regarded with such contempt and because of his reputation as a Maskil (and probably, although Abramovitsh doesn't say this, because he feared recriminations for his powerful satire), he submitted the story anonymously, but presented by a fictional narrator named Senderel Mocher Seforim. Tzederboim, however, fearing that readers would think he wrote the story (Senderel being a Yiddish diminutive form of Alexander), changed the narrator's name to Mendele Mocher Seforim. Thus, at least according to Abramovitsh, was born the fictional character whose identity soon overshadowed the real identity of his creator.

Although *Dos Kleyne Mentshele* began as a short story, Abramovitsh, a tireless reviser of his own works in his search for perfection, expanded and rewrote it in 1879 and then revised it again in 1907. The following discussion of the novel will be based on the 1907 version and the 1879 introduction[4] which is an important introduction to the character of Mendele.

Mendele is a narrator who loves digressions, and his introduction actually begins with a digression, a discussion of the Jewish habit of always asking a stranger his name. Mendele seems to be critical of this habit—after all, whose business is it to pry into a stranger's name?—but the discussion actually leads up to Mendele's disclosure of his own name and then into a self-description, including information about his place and date of birth, his physical appearance, his previous and present occupations, and his family. After this introduction, Mendele launches right into his story.

One autumn day in 1855, traveling with his horse and wagonload of stock through the various Jewish communities, he came to a fork in the road, and, unable to decide which road to take, he imitated Don Quixote and numerous other knights errant and allowed his horse to make the choice. The horse chose the road to Glupsk (Foolstown, the Yiddish Version of Kesalon), and Mendele was happy enough to go there. When he arrived in town, however, he found everything in confusion because of the recent death of one of the town's most important citizens, Yitzchok-Avrom Bigwig. Shortly after his arrival, he was called to the home of the town's rabbi, where the rabbi explained that Yitzchok-Avrom had left a long confession, part of which the rabbi had already read to the town leaders. Would Mendele, he asked, please read that part and then come back the next morning to hear the conclusion? Mendele, relieved that he was not in trouble himself, consented and, having taken care of his horse, immediately began reading.

The confession itself, in which Yitzchok-Avrom tells the story of his life, forms the body of the novel. Because he was born into a poor family and because his father soon died, Yitzchok-Avrom grew up in terrible conditions, which he describes in some detail. The overriding fact about his childhood is that it was characterized by a lack of love. Poverty and his mother's need to work deprived him of familial love; the incompetence of his teacher in the Talmud Torah[5] removed love from any aspect of education; and the general tenor of *shtetl* life made his various apprenticeships into horrifying experiences. At different times he worked in a general store, was apprentice to a tailor and a shoemaker, and was a chorus boy for a traveling cantor; and each experience was characterized by hunger, beatings, and rejection, until finally the cantor abandoned him in the town of Tsvuatshitz. Here the friendless and frightened boy was treated kindly by Jacobson, who subsequently introduced him to Gutman (Yiddish for Goodman). Gutman, a Maskil of the same sort as Abramovitsh, was religious, but he had shaved his beard and wore modern clothes. Although a dedicated, hard worker, he was poor, and the community leaders scorned his work. Clearly he was a "good man" and he took the boy on as a helper.

At this point, the manuscript which the rabbi gave Mendele ended, and he was forced to wait until morning to hear the end. In the morning all the town leaders, clearly a disreputable group, were gathered in the rabbi's study. The rabbi came in and began the reading. Yitzchok-Avrom's position with Gutman marked the happiest time of his life, but because he was dissatisfied with Gutman's poverty, he decided to study the lives of rich men. First he got a job in the house of Dr. Steinhartz (Stoneheart), a rich doctor who made money by cheating his patients. Overhearing the doctor's conversations with the equally dishonest druggist, Yitzchok-Avrom began to learn the way to become rich; and when he later took a job with another charlatan, the community leader Issar Varger (Issar the Strangler), he learned all there was to know about becoming rich by being a bloodsucking parasite, by fooling and taking advantage of the town's poor people, and by raising and collecting taxes.

Yitzchok-Avrom, imitating Issar Varger, began to make money. He also fell in love with Golda Jacobson, the pure, good daughter of the man who had helped him in Tsvuashitz and who had recently died, leaving his family in extreme poverty. Their one consolation was Michael, Golda's fiancé, who, through Yitzchok-Avrom's connivance, was drafted and sent away, thus clearing the way for Yitzchok-Avrom to marry Golda. (Obviously this is not the kind of pure romantic love we saw in *Ha'avot Vehabanim*.) Shortly after the wedding, however, Yitzchok-Avrom regretted the drain on his finances brought on by the marriage and began abusing Golda and her mother. When he lost his job with Issar, and his mother-in-law died, he left Golda and went to Glupsk, where be became well known and was soon offered a match with the ugly daughter of the town's richest man. Attracted by wealth and social standing, he did not tell them of his earlier marriage, but sneaked back to Tsvuashitz and divorced Golda, leaving her alone with their infant son. Because of his new connections in Glupsk, and following Issar Varger's advice, he soon became a success, the town's leading citizen. Shortly before his death, however, he began to realize that he was still friendless and unloved, that all his wealth was useless, and that he had sinned terribly in amassing it.

From here to the end his confession is overtly didactic. First he presents a list of his sins, accompanied by a thorough description of them. He then describes his gradual reformation, at the same time criticizing the typical Talmud Torah education offered to the poor and lamenting the scorn shown for manual labor. This section is followed by several specific requests, which are to be aided by money left in his will: first, the town should build a new Talmud Torah and a vocational school, both of which should employ modern educational methods and should teach secular subjects; second, the schools should be headed by the rabbi and by Gutman, if he can be found; and third, Yitzchok-Avrom's story should be published and distributed by Mendele so that other community leaders, as well as the leaders of Glupsk who had just heard it, might learn from it. Of course the leaders of Glupsk were outraged, finally having understood that the confession was directed at them, and they stormed out; but Mendele agreed to do what Yitzchok-Avrom has asked of him. The book ends with the news that Mendele has been unable to find Gutman, but if anyone knows where he is, it would be praiseworthy to send him to Glupsk.

What even a lengthy summary like this is unable to capture, however, is the satiric tone of the work. For one thing, whenever there was a pause in the reading—and the rabbi was often interrupted by people asking advice on various matters—Mendele would either record the conversations of the leaders who were in the room with him or describe the cause of the interruption. These digressions, as we shall see, always bear an important relation to Yitzchok-Avrom's narrative. Second, the novel, like other picaresque novels to which it is closely related, is often very funny, both in its satire and in the kinds of adventures that Yitzchok-Avrom lives through.

Obviously *Dos Kleyne Mentshele* is a very different kind of book from *Ha'avot Vehabanim*. Abramovitsh did not simply switch languages but changed the whole focus of his work, and this change is underlined by his use of the picaresque form. The picaresque novel had arisen in sixteenth century Spain under conditions very much like those that Abramovitsh saw in his own people. In the sixteenth century, Spain had become a nation full of corruption; its high church and governmental leaders were either dishonest or incompetent, and a sense of physical and spiritual poverty had enervated the common people. The anonymous author of the first picaresque novel, *Lazarillo de Tormes*, surveyed the situation throughout the country by having his hero take part in a series of discrete adventures satirizing every social caste. Thus, by the end of the novel we have been given realistic descriptions of beggars, workmen, clergymen, women, and the nobility; and in every case we have been shown some combination of poverty and moral bankruptcy. Throughout, Lazarillo is victimized by all the characters he describes, and though he occasionally gets some revenge, we are most aware of his constant hunger and the beatings he receives at the hands of his master. At the end of the novel, although Lazarillo has reached a position of some security, he can only keep it by becoming, like the people he condemns, a self-deceptive hypocrite. Using the pattern established in *Lazarillo de Tormes*, writers from other times and other countries have surveyed and satirized their own cultures, manipulating many of the conventions to suit their purposes but keeping the general form of a journey through the different layers of society. Usually this journey takes the form of a biography or an autobiography, though, as Ronald Paulson says, "What appears to be a man's life . . . is in fact a series of discrete relationships that serve as devices of satiric exposition."[6] This is the case with *Dos Kleyne Mentshele*. By following Yitzchok-Avrom's adventures with his teachers, masters, guardians, and fellow parasites, we can see the whole of Eastern European Jewish life in the mid-nineteenth century; and we can agree with Yitzchok-Avrom when he says that his crimes "were not only my own crimes, the crimes of an individual, but in large part—perhaps for the most part—they were attributable to society and its evil customs" (164). The satire directed against communal leaders like Yitzchok-Avrom is bitter indeed, but Abramovitsh does not hold them solely responsible for the troubles of the Jewish people. They are, after all, the product of their environment—the product of poverty, lack of education, and scorn for physical labor. Thus Yitzchok-Avrom's will provides both for the education of the leaders through publication of his confession and for the improvement of the environment through the establishment of good schools. And while many of the individual scenes in the novel are humorous, the overall effect created by these realistic pictures of everyday life is horrifying, as it is in so many picaresque novels. Abramovitsh's satire, like most good satire, is not merely funny, it is also disturbing; and we must now examine what made—and still makes—*Dos Kleyne Mentshele* so disturbing.

II   *Surveying the* Shtetl

One of the most impressive aspects of the novel is its sense of realism. This does not stem simply from our knowledge that Glupsk—Foolstown—is really Berdichev, the city where Abramovitsh lived, or that Yitzchok-Avrom is based "on a living person, who at that time had only to snap his whip in Glupsk in order to drive the whole congregation of Israel."[7] Although Abramovitsh predated the great Naturalists of the late nineteenth century, we feel, as we read about Layzer the Tailor or about Yitzchok-Avrom's teacher, that these characters in fact represent the general level of workmen and teachers, because even in their brief appearances in the book they seem so lifelike. This sense of realism is enhanced by the objectivity of these descriptions. Yitzchok-Avrom, having no friend to confess to, has written down his confession for his own benefit in complete honesty. Since he is so frank about his own sins and shortcomings, we tend to trust his evaluations of other characters. As Paulson says, in *Lazarillo* and other picaresque novels, "the reader tends to associate himself with the confidential, likable first-person speaker—or rather he is tricked into doing so—but becomes increasingly aware of the protagonist's (and therefore his own) shortcomings."[8] But whereas Lazarillo deceives himself and denies his shortcomings, Yitzchok-Avrom announces his publicly. Although we may not identify with him as closely as with other picaresque heroes, his frank confession earns our respect and persuades us to accept what he says as true. Furthermore, the acceptance and presentation of Yitzchok-Avrom's confession by that cynical, suspicious man of the world Mendele Mocher Seforim makes us even more receptive to Yitzchok-Avrom's descriptions and evaluations, a receptiveness that is further reinforced by Mendele's own realistic descriptions of his arrival in Glupsk and of the various people who enter the rabbi's study during the reading of the confession.

Part of the book's horror derives from the evolution of the words "dos kleyne mentshele," which literally mean "the little man." Stillman's translation of the book's title as *The Parasite* reflects the implications of the term by the novel's end, but overlooks the term's shift in meaning from its first appearance: when Yitzchok-Avrom was a little boy, he looked into his mother's eyes and, seeing his own reflection, asked " 'Mama! Who is the little man in your eyes?' " His mother's answer presents one of the phrase's meanings: " 'My little fool! The little man is the soul,' " and Yitzchok-Avrom records that in his childish simplicity, "I developed a great desire to be a little man myself. Can you imagine—the little man is a soul! In size no bigger than a flea, and yet in him is concentrated the gist, the very kernel of life!" (36). What Yitzchok-Avrom failed to realize was that he was seeing himself, his reflection, and that his description of the little man was a description of himself as an independent human being in whom was concentrated "the gist, the very kernel of life."

Yitzchok-Avrom's flawed understanding of the term became more confused when he overheard two conversations between Jacobson and Gutman. In one, Gutman told Jacobson that " 'Dr. Steinhartz is a little man and that is why he is so rich and leads others by the nose. Is it news to you? It stands to reason that if one becomes a little man, he can accomplish anything in the world' " (79). In the second conversation, Gutman described Issar Varger as " 'the very soul of the local magnate.' "[9] Gutman, of course, was using the term to mean something like a parasite, but Yitzchok-Avrom, with his conception of the little man as the soul (a conception reinforced by Gutman's description of Issar Varger), wanted more than ever to become one, since apparently being a little man would lead to wealth and happiness. In a prophetic dream, he saw a little man (in the literal sense) walking down the street and engaged in various tricks, the kind of tricks that he, as a parasite, would later employ himself: collaborating with tax collectors, stealing from the community treasury, and fixing the price of meat to take advantage of the poor. In his dream, Yitzchok-Avrom even became a little man: "Soon I became the soul, the very life of several important people and my fortune started rising" (82). When he awoke, however, and analyzed his dream, he discovered that "one cannot become a little man unless one stops thinking and feeling. One must not think or feel regardless of another person's pain or misery" (83), and it became his goal to learn how to accomplish this task, to cut himself off from humanity.

His last confusion about what it meant to be a little man disappeared after he went to work for Dr. Steinhartz, who, in spite of Gutman's description of him as "a little man," was, to the boy's surprise, physically huge. Finally, having studied the doctor's methods, Yitzchok-Avrom discovered that "one can remain full size while one is a little man. To be a little man, one must be a parasite, a bloodsucker, and cheat others of their money" (90). Thus, his understanding of the term became exactly the opposite of what it had been. Originally thinking of the little man as the soul, that which distinguishes man from all other creatures (his mother had said that animals have no "little men" in their eyes), he now thought of the little man as an unthinking, unfeeling parasite, a creature in human form lacking precisely those characteristics that distinguish human beings from other forms of life. The little man, though created by his social environment, perpetuates that environment and insures that he will be followed by other little men. To show this, Abramovitsh has Yitzchok-Avrom use terms related to religious studies when he describes what he learned from Issar Varger: "I thoroughly reviewed all the rules and regulations of being a little man, together with Issar's commentaries and my own annotations" (135), and "Issar's word was for me a Torah."[10] As Yitzchok-Avrom reviewed the overall situation, he saw that the corruption that characterized Jewish life in the *shtetl* had become more than a temporary evil, that it had taken on the force of tradition. In Jewish life this means that it also may have something of the force of religion behind it, especially for people who are not fully aware of what their religion means— because they learned about their religion in the kind of Talmud Torah that Yitzchok-Avrom condemned. The misery was self-perpetuating, and his confession was an attempt to break the cycle; but obviously the rich men, the community leaders, who gathered to hear the confession relied on the cycle's continuation for their own success.

These community leaders, the main satiric targets of Abramovitsh's first two Yiddish works, were all "little men," hypocrites who pretended to be acting in the people's behalf while really taking advantage of them. Their hypocrisy is evident from the very beginning, when Mendele overhears a conversation between two of the mourners. One of the rich men had just been lamenting Yitzchok-Avrom's death in the most pitying terms, when another said to him

> "Tell me, Laybtsheh, what was it that you said a while ago?"
> "What I said a while ago? I? What *did* I say, Yossel? Really, what did. . . ."
> "Certainly, certainly! You yourself, with your kosher little mouth! Didn't you say: 'Is he also a human being, this Itzik-Avreml the Strong-arm Man? He was, he may pardon me or not, a ruffian, a leech, a swindler, a liar, a brute and, to top it off, a lecher?' " (27–28)

Their hypocrisy and their lack of human feeling were also evident when Mendele saw them in the rabbi's study. None of them really cared about their supposed friend—they mourned his death only because he had been so useful to them, because his death would have a bad effect on " 'the city, on us, that is,' "[11] as one of them said. Like corrupt leaders from all ages, they equated their own welfare with the welfare of the city, which means that they ran the city government only in order to benefit themselves. Everyone else may suffer—as long as the wealthy leaders can become wealthier, they are fully satisfied. Thus their conversation quickly shifted from the death of their friend to one's desire to get away so he could make some extra money for doing something that should be a community service, to another's hunger, and to a third's problem with his hemorrhoids (a problem which affects many of Abramovitsh's villains). This progression from moneymaking to piles underlines not only their selfishness, but also their ultimate absurdity, their real littleness. Their success was based on illusion and a lack of humanity, not on learning or merit. The only power they had was what they could convince the people to give them. Unfortunately, the people were gullible and gave them as much power as they wanted.

All of these qualities of the "little men," the wealthy community leaders, are illustrated in Yitzchok-Avrom's descriptions of the two "little men" for whom he worked, Dr. Steinhartz and Issar Varger. Dr. Steinhartz was a big, coarse man who addressed Yitzchok-Avrom only in Russian, calling him "jackass" and "fool" and thereby teaching the boy how a rich man should treat his underlings. Even more important, however, is what Yitzchok-Avrom learned from eavesdropping on a conversation between the doctor and Getzl the apothecary, in which the two men discussed how they conspired to cheat patients by treating imaginary ills. Significantly, the main topic of their conversation was treatment with leeches, for they themselves were leeches, bloodsuckers, parasites, people who drained the community by overtreating the rich and neglecting the poor.

Even worse was Issar Varger, whose power was based entirely on illusion. Barely able to read and write, he had convinced everyone that he was learned and had high government connections. His attitude toward his people is obvious in his conversation with a friend:

"I tell you that in the whole wide world there is no people so dear, so good as the Jews. Really, a good people, a golden people. Upon my faith, they will give you their last—groschen!"
"It would be better, Issar, to say a foolish people. Such fools as Jews don't exist anywhere else in the world!"
"Correct, brother o' mine! What's true is true. There is no other people, so good, so useful, so golden, and so foolish as our brothers! There just isn't!" (94–95)

In his view, the people were there to be taken advantage of, and unfortunately they allowed themselves to be victimized. Their protest against a higher tax on kosher meat, for example, was quelled when Issar warned them to accept the tax lest the tax collector resign. " 'If you think I knew what I was talking about,' reported Issar to his friend, 'you're mistaken' "; but the people " 'agreed to everything. The prices were raised even more than I had expected and everybody left in an elated mood' " (95–96). Issar was a fraud and a charlatan, but the people, convinced that he was powerful, gave him power, agreed to their own destruction, allowed him to overtax them and keep the surplus himself.

These were Yitzchok-Avrom's teachers, and Yitzchok-Avrom proved a good student. His earliest sins on the road to becoming a "little man" involved his marriage. First, in order to marry Golda, he paid to have Michael drafted and sent away; and after the marriage he became such a terrible miser that Golda had to beg him for money. Perhaps he can be said to have attained "little manhood" by his behavior at the death of Golda's mother: "Golda and Shayndeleh [her sister] wailed so pitifully that a stone would have turned. I covered my face with both hands, and, although it is a foul and shameful thing to admit, smiled with pleasure, having just been rid of a heavy burden" (139). Hypocrisy, greed, and a lack of concern for anyone else had all become permanent parts of his character. Consequently, it was no problem for him to return to Tsvuatshitz from Glupsk and divorce Golda, in one of the novel's most pathetic scenes, nor did he have any trouble becoming one of the leading citizens of Glupsk. With Issar's methods and his own intelligence— intelligence that he himself says should have been put to better use—it was an easy task for him to make his way in the world.

The novel reaches its climax, however, in an extraordinary chapter, that part of his manuscript in which he comments on all his previous actions while convincing us of his new-found honesty. The chapter appears to open with an account of his easy successes in Glupsk, thanks to his rich new father-in-law, but he soon says, "My confession will make you understand a tenth of a tenth of my way, my course of action in my life."[12] This is followed by a long list of his sins, a list that uses the form of the confession that every Jew recites a number of times on the Day of Atonement. The religious confession begins

> For the sin which we have committed before Thee
> under compulsion or of our own will;
> And for the sin which we have committed before Thee
> in hardening of the heart;
> For the sin which we have committed before Thee
> unknowingly;
> And for the sin which we have committed before Thee
> with utterance of the lips. . . .[13]

Yitzchok-Avrom's confession inserts a paragraph of explanation after each sin, but the confession itself includes such matters as

> For the sin which I committed in being a little man. . . .
> And for the sin which I committed in being a leaseholder. . . .
> For the sin which I committed in using hocus-pocus. . . .
> And for the sin which I committed in matters of taxes. . . .[14]

This lengthy confession enables Yitzchok-Avrom both to relieve his tortured conscience and to expose more thoroughly the techniques

employed by the "little men" to keep their fellow Jews in a state of
subjugation. Among the crimes that he confessed to were blackmail,
election fixing, and manipulation of religious laws for his own profit.

We feel that Yitzchok-Avrom's repentance was real, and we know
that his proposal for modern education might succeed in eliminating
some of the evils he has discussed; but we also know that his proposal will probably never become a reality, because, in commenting
on: "And I sinned in the Misuse of the Fear of the Lord," he himself
said: "Whenever anything was suggested to better the life of the
people, I and my crowd promptly labeled it as a scheme of the devil
and exerted all our cunning to eliminate the plague. We considered
it an infernal scheme, for example, that Jewish children should be
taught to read, write, and figure in order to earn an honorable
livelihood" (153). This view was reflected in the reactions of the
town leaders when the rabbi finished reading the confession: " 'No,
no, Rabbi!' several gentlemen protested with deeply offended
voices. 'This is unprecedented! To tell people such things right to
their faces! Where is justice? To make people into . . . into . . . who
asked him to do it? Speak for yourself, write for yourself, but what
business is it of yours to pick others apart? What right do you have to
delve into other's. . . . No, Rabbi. It's a great injustice' " (170–71).
We know, of course, the reasons behind their immediate outrage—
their methods have been exposed and the suggestion has been made
"to better the life of the people." Nevertheless, they were still in
power, and between their efforts and the disappearance of Gutman,
Yitzchok-Avrom's proposal seemed doomed. Mendele's concluding
announcement that anyone knowing Gutman's whereabouts should
send him to Glupsk is also Abramovitsh's plea that any "good man"
should come—to Berdichev, to every Jewish town—and rescue the
people from their leaders. He is doing his part by satirizing them in
his book, by opening the people's eyes to their real situation, but he
needs every "good man" to rise up with him.

Abramovitsh's treatment of Gutman illustrates his attitude toward
the Haskala at this point in his career. He still felt that education
would be the saving force in the history of his people, and some of
Yitzchok-Avrom's bitterest remarks were directed at the school he
attended: "I studied in the *Talmud-Torah*. Everyone knows what a
Talmud-Torah is, so that it is really unnecessary to describe it. It is a
grave in which poor Jewish children are buried, where their minds
are mutilated and where they are removed from all contact with the

world in which they live. It is a factory that manufactures good-for-nothings, ne'er-do-wells, and spineless, unfortunate creatures. It is a vast pit, an abyss, an unclean hovel standing on wobbly supports . . ." (37). Instead of educating, bringing light and life to students, the Talmud Torah stifled their curiosity and consigned them to lives of ignorance and continued poverty. Much of this resulted from the general poverty of the community, but the teachers were also culpable: "The *rebbeh* [teacher], who by no means deserved the title Rabbi, was enchanted by one subject—beatings. . . ." And later Yitzchok-Avrom adds: "They killed in me the feeling of human dignity, of the value and worth of the human being . . ." (37, 87, 164),[15] precisely those elements on which Judaism is founded. Nevertheless, Abramovitsh did not see education and traditional religion as adversaries, as so many other Maskilim tended to do. Thus, one of Gutman's key scenes in the book concerned his having to sell his overcoat so that his family could make provision for Passover. As he explained to his wife, " 'We are still better off than the others, who have become rich through swindles and who make provisions for our sacred religious holiday with money earned by non-kosher means.' "[16] For Abramovitsh, the Haskala and the Jewish religion went hand in hand; and although he discarded some traditional customs—that of wearing old-fashioned clothes, for instance—he adhered to his religion. Thus Yitzchok-Avrom's will provided for good secular and religious education, and Gutman and the rabbi, Haskala and religion, were to be partners. The people had to be introduced to worldly subjects such as the sciences and foreign languages, and they also needed a better religious education in order to eradicate their tendency to superstition. As Yitzchok-Avrom said, his conception of sin had included such items as not believing in good and bad spirits, not believing that ghosts pray in the synagogue at night, and not believing in reincarnation. Such superstitions obscured true religious beliefs and enabled unscrupulous leaders to prey on their ignorance. (Even Mendele counts wolves' teeth and amulets among his wares.) The rabbi, like Gutman, was clearly a good man, for knowing that Yitzchok-Avrom was telling the truth, he yet had the courage to read the accusatory confession to the leaders; but, again, he could do little alone. However, through the uniting of the religious and the secular, Jewish life would be able to enter the modern world while still retaining its Jewishness. All that was needed was modern education, training

that would open the people's eyes both to the outside world and to
their own subjugation. Although Abramovitsh was to modify this
view in later works, especially in *Di Klyatshe*, it is significant that he
let it stand even in the last revision of *Dos Kleyne Mentshele*, for it
represented an important ideal in his career and in the history of the
Haskala.

In addition to examining the community leaders, the Haskala,
and the religious life, *Dos Kleyne Mentshele* looks at the lives of the
common people, the people whose cause Abramovitsh championed
throughout his life. He was always very much concerned with the
lower classes (though he would never have used the term); indeed
one of his greatest novels, *Fishke der Krumer*, concentrates on the
lives of beggars. *Dos Kleyne Mentshele*, however, concentrates on
the poor working class. Abramovitsh was disturbed that honest
manual labor as well as skilled labor had fallen into disrepute. Thus
he has Yitzchok-Avrom's mother say, " 'Better should he perish
than to go and work with his hands, disgracing me and his father
lying in his grave. . . . What do you think—Reb Tevil the
Melamed's son should become an apprentice to a handworker? It
hurts me even to think of it' " (40–41). Her attitude reflected the
change that had occurred in the Jewish outlook over the centuries,
for in earlier times the importance of labor was recognized. Even
Rashi, the great eleventh century commentator on the Bible,
earned his livelihood by keeping a vineyard. In the nineteenth century, however, manual labor among the Jews, because of both internal and external pressures, was looked upon with scorn. When
Yitzchok-Avrom finally was apprenticed to various masters, his descriptions of them and their treatment of him help to explain the
problem.

Yitzchok-Avrom's first master was Layzer the tailor, under whose
tutelage "I worked like a horse and was beaten from every quarter.
At that time I was under the impression that it was necessary to treat
an apprentice in such a fashion, else he would never become a good
worker . . ." (53). Even more important, however, the boy was
never taught anything about tailoring. Here—and with his other
masters as well—his apprenticeship consisted of household chores,
babysitting, and marketing; and he was constantly exposed to the
violence of a life lived without either physical or spiritual wealth:
"Sometimes Layzer would beat me and sometimes his wife would
take a hand, and sometimes both of them beat me together. At times

they would beat me in the following manner: Layzer would send a few stinging slaps in his wife's direction; she would forward them to me with interest, on occasion throwing in a few pinches as a bonus. At other times, Mrs. Layzer would, with her own hands, invest as many blows as her strength would allow in Layzer, and he, not being able to bear it, would reinvest them all in me" (52). Yitzchok-Avrom's use of economic terms in this passage is significant, for such was the poverty in which he lived that he could talk about his suffering only in relation to interest and bonuses. This is not the happy, romanticized world of *Fiddler on the Roof*. This is the harsh reality, the poverty, the emptiness that Abramovitsh saw afflicting Jewish life. Still, he could not blame the workers. In a lengthy comment at the end of the confession, he had Yitzchok-Avrom say:

> Working with one's hands has fallen into terrible disrepute among Jews. Just as a ne'er-do-well, a parasite, is regarded as a swindler, so is the craftsman regarded as a blot on the family honor. Anyone who by any stretch of the imagination can call himself an independent businessman, although his belly be swollen with hunger, will not teach his children a trade that is even remotely connected with handwork. For this type of work God has provided enough castaway orphans, children of the lowly common people. . . . The apprenticeship generally starts with the dirtiest work: carrying the slop-pails, fetching water from the well, guarding the baby. . . . For dessert, the apprentice is privileged to listen to the vile language current among handworkers, love stories with pornographic twists, which will almost certainly extinguish any remnant glowing embers of human feeling that may accidentally have survived in him. . . .
>
> Nor is it entirely the fault of the handworkers. They, just like me and thousands of other poor children, have led bitter lives. They, too, started by carrying pails of slop and garbage. (165)

The whole economic structure of the *shtetl* needed revision. The Steinhartzes and Issar Vargers, who were respected for doing nothing, had to be deposed, while the dignity of the workmen who really made the city run had to be raised. Again Abramovitsh's answer was education: good vocational schools with competent teachers should be established, so that apprentices may "learn to be well-educated craftsmen who will know their own worth and who will therefore be able to compel others to appreciate and understand their value" (166).

But, if the working class was downtrodden and despised, women were in an even worse position. In his survey of Jewish life in the midnineteenth century, Abramovitsh raised questions about women's roles that are still being discussed. For example, Yitzchok-Avrom's mother does not play a large part in the novel and she is not very fully described, but her difficulty in caring for her family after her husband's death prompts her son to make the following observation: "A woman's work has no value in our world and is but scantily rewarded. For what is a woman anyway? What is the worth of the whole woman? What kind of respect does she command even if she is an exceptionally capable housewife? Women, so the whole world believes, will never amount to anything. None of their jobs have any solid foundations. Work that requires deep thought, and is useful as well, is not for a woman's mind" (40). It would be difficult to find a better summary of the lot of Jewish women in Eastern Europe, which, like that of the workers, indicated the extent to which *shtetl* life had moved from the essence of Judaism. If Yitzchok-Avrom thought he had lost respect for human dignity, the whole environment conspired against the dignity of women. They could only hold the meanest of jobs, like plucking chickens, darning socks, or, like Golda when Yitzchok-Avrom met her, taking in mending. They were entirely dependent on men for whatever they had, which still was not much. One of the major indications in the confession of women's position was the way in which Yitzchok-Avrom could divorce Golda for no good reason, with no consultation, and with no legal responsibility to support her or their infant son; and she was practically powerless to stop him.

This picture from the confession is reinforced by matters that come up during interruptions in the rabbi's reading. The first concerns a woman whose husband, a Hasid, mistreated her terribly. Most of the time he was away from home with his *tzaddik*; and when he was home, he abused her, refusing to support her financially. Finally, when she complained to him, he threatened: " 'I will cast you off forever and make you an outcast, deserted woman. I'll remarry somewhere again—I'm allowed to, it's my privilege. I must teach you a lesson. You'll learn your place!' " (114). She has come to the rabbi seeking a divorce, which, though it may be hard for us to realize today, was a drastic move. A woman without a husband faced terrible hardships, but the Hasidic treatment of women made that hardship the lesser of the two evils. Abramovitsh did not generally attack the Hasidim (as other Maskilic authors did) for he wanted to bring Jews closer together, not drive them apart. In terms of interpersonal relationships, however, the Hasidic treatment of women, which had in many ways become part of Jewish culture, needed reform. After all, Yitzchok-Avrom's treatment of Golda was very much like the Hasid's treatment of his wife; and in both cases women were seen as being something less than human.

The most significant commentary on the bitterness of women's lives, however, came from the rabbi's wife, during another interruption in the reading. Mendele had just offered her a gift, a book of Yiddish lamentations written especially for women, and in the course of thanking him she mentioned the male view that women " 'have no souls. Women are not human and need nothing. They should be satisfied with the fact that they live, bear children and raise them, cook meals, take care of their husbands, and lead a miserable existence.' " Mendele's answer is significant: " 'Praised be God that we see each other again in the best of health. . . . I think we've done enough for the women folk.' " First he ignored her complaint, then denied its validity. In this he was backed up by the town leaders, who overheard the conversation, and there follows one of the most amazing interchanges in Yiddish literature, between the leaders and the rabbi's wife. First one of them asks her why it says " 'in one of our holy works that the entire wisdom possessed by woman is the knowledge of operating the spinning wheel.' " She replies that it is " 'because the book was written by a man. Of course, you are the clever ones. You have the power and you hold womankind in the palms of your hands. The strong one is always the clever one, the righteous one' " (66). Then, when Mendele assures her that she will enjoy the book of lamentations (called in Yiddish a *Techina*), she responds:

True, Reb Mendele. . . . For us poor women *Techinas* are good. They are the only remedies for hearts that are full of boils and wounds. At least they make us weep; they allow us to empty the bitter dregs of our hearts in the flowing streams of our warm tears. But it's vexing, it's exasperating to see how the menfolk, who don't understand and have no desire to understand the turmoil within us, scoff at and joke about the women's *Techinas* and begrudge us even this remedy. Let them sit in the women's gallery of the synagogue on the Sabbath or on a holiday . . . one woman sits oppressed by the dark fate that has cursed her with such a husband; another is a desolate divorcee; still another has an embittered countenance because of

her sick suckling child . . . a fourth has swollen, scalded hands from standing at the oven all day; a fifth has a pale face and a worried look because of
her continual serfdom, from endlessly plodding in the harness. (67–68)

When the rabbi's wife had finished her revolutionary statement and
left the room, Mendele found himself very much affected by her
words. The cockiness and self-assurance of his previous answer to
her disappeared as he began to recognize the kind of terror that
women had to face throughout their lives; and the more he thought,
the more pity he had for them, until he came to an important
realization about himself, women, and Jews in general: "This, I
figure, is what a good, learned, non-Jew must feel when he begins to
think about the situation of the Jews, to reckon their value, to regret
the troubles which they, though weak, must bear from the gentile
nations, their strong masters."[17] The social criticism contained in
this statement can be viewed in two parallel contexts. On the one
hand, it is tragic that the Jews suffer so much because of the gentile
nations, who view the Jews as subhuman, worthless creatures. On
the other hand, with this ever present example, it is unfortunate
that the Jews themselves treat the female half of their population
unfairly. Certainly, according to Abramovitsh, the Jews were
downtrodden, victimized by every other nation, but this was all the
more reason for them to avoid making the same mistakes. Men who
take advantage of women are as parasitical, as "little-man-like," as
any of the community leaders. Jewish women were in a sorry state,
but a state that Abramovitsh hoped to remedy by calling attention to
it.[18]

III   *The Denunciation of the Beloved*

Dos Kleyne Mentshele, then, offers a thorough survey of the
shtetl's social classes, from the top to the bottom, showing how they
all contribute to and suffer from the general misery in which the
Jews as a whole lived. Abramovitsh's basic solution lay in education,
but he did not mean by this the learning of facts, laws, and skills,
though these were certainly important. Even more important, however, was the necessity of learning how to be human, of recognizing
one's own humanity and the humanity of others, not only so that
"little men"—parasites—would not be able to survive, but so that
no one would feel the need to be one. The difficulty of this task, if
not self-evident, is emphasized by the character of Mendele. At the

beginning he was cocky and cynical, attitudes that were reflected in his self-description. Thus, for example, he told us that among his wares were "storybooks, including a few of the more modern novels," the religious goods that he would be expected to carry, as well as "wolves' teeth" and amulets (22).[19] In his role as a merchant, he had no principles: he could sell novels, which represented the Haskala, or amulets, which represented the most backward kind of superstition. He could also play games with his readers: one of the best examples of this is what Miron calls the " 'this is beside the point' trick," in which Mendele would say something that seemed totally off his main topic, ending his comment by saying, "This is beside the point." For example, when he first arrived in Glupsk, "I was very curious to know what was going on. . . . One should know about everything that goes on in the world. One can never tell when this knowledge will be useful. There is many a Jew who earns his daily bread by prodding his nose into every pot and sniffing: wherever there are two partners, he barges in to make a third and demands his share. Being united is a Jewish trait. But this is beside the point" (27).[20] Not only is his comment about unity ironic in its immediate context, but the rest of the novel will prove that it is ironic in the whole context of Jewish life: a large part of the Jews' problems stemmed from their lack of unity. Far from being "beside the point," it is exactly the point, as both Mendele and Abramovitsh knew.

But this knowledge had little effect on Mendele, for he found that in order to live in the world, he had to be like the world. Thus, when he was first called to the rabbi's study, he was afraid that his daughter's father-in-law was charging him with not living up to the terms of the marriage contract, terms that Mendele indicates that he never intended to fulfill. Furthermore, in commenting on his job and on the rabbi, he said things like, "The world insists that one be a cheat," "The whole world is a market," and "In the world one must practice deception."[21] In short, Mendele's views and practices were not terribly distinct from those of an Issar Varger. And if Mendele appears to be like the "little men," it is important to realize that the name Mendele is a diminutive form of a word for man, in other words, a "little man."[22] To say this is not necessarily to condemn Mendele. It is, rather, to acknowledge the difficulty of the task that Abramovitsh (through Yitzchok-Avrom's will) has set for the Jews. It is, as Miron says, "a timely reminder, that it is easier to recommend perfect honesty from the vantage point of a deathbed than from that of the daily struggle for bread."[23] Education was still Abramovitsh's ideal solution, but he required an education that must change the whole person, the community, even the human character. With all of Mendele's cynicism, his acceptance of cheating as a necessity, he was still moved by what the rabbi's wife said, and we know that his attitude toward women became radically different from what it had been. We know, too, that the rabbi's wife focused his attention more clearly on the plight of the Jews. And finally, we know that Mendele undertook, at great inconvenience to himself, to fulfill the terms of Yitzchok-Avrom's will. He published the confession; he tried to find Gutman; and he tried to convey the full import of the confession to the Jewish people. His concluding announcement is free of cynicism and irony—it is important that Gutman be found so that the school can be started. "Take pity, ladies and gentlemen!" he wrote, "Do it for the sake of poor Jewish children" (172). Although Mendele knew the ways of the world, he also knew that the world could be better.

Mendele's cynicism, then, functions in several ways. First, it is a protective device that Mendele used to cover up the fact that he had to follow the ways of the world, even if it meant being somewhat like the "little men." Second, it allowed Abramovitsh to convey his message more effectively by making Mendele less overtly didactic. He did not let Mendele sermonize, but he made his points more effectively by having Mendele's cynicism pierced by the rabbi's wife and by Mendele himself at the novel's end; and though Mendele's cynicism always returns, we know that there is a big difference between his cynicism, his cutting insights into the lives of the common people, and the absolute scorn with which he looked upon the corrupt town leaders. And third, as Miron points out, it enabled Abramovitsh to distance himself from the story, to show Mendele's development as a character, to make his work artistic and emotionally appealing. Though he recognized their flaws, Abramovitsh clearly loved his fellow Jews. He sympathized with their misery, though he realized that much of that misery was self-imposed. He had to chastise his people as a parent chastises a favorite child, denouncing their faults but making his love obvious at the same time. This is what Abramovitsh did, with Mendele's help, in *Dos Kleyne Mentshele*.

IV *Significance of* Dos Kleyne Mentshele

Unquestionably, *Dos Kleyne Mentshele* is an important book in the history of Yiddish literature: its compassion, its realism (though many of the minor characters are really caricatures), its thoughtful use of the Yiddish language—these elements all make the book historically significant. But the novel is also important from standpoints other than literary history. It is a well-constructed picaresque novel, fully in line with the picaresque tradition, and it is a significant commentary on the life of the Jews in Eastern Europe in the nineteenth century. It may not be a particularly pleasant work, showing as it does the seamier side of Jewish life, but as Stuart Miller says: "The picaresque novel is ugly; it speaks of the possibilities of human degradation rather than of human triumph."[24] And if the novel seems didactic today, it is far less so than were its Yiddish predecessors: as we saw, earlier Yiddish writers who were also Maskilim tended to write not for literary or artistic purposes but in order to bring about reforms.[25] By combining artistry with didacticism his social commentary becomes even more striking: for example, in the interplay among Yitzchok-Avrom, the community leaders, the rabbi and Mendele.

His artistry is apparent, too, in his use of Jewish references. Thus, Yitzchok-Avrom saw Golda for the first time on Sabbath Nachamu—the Sabbath after the fast of the Ninth of Ab, the solemn commemoration of the destruction of the first and second temples. This Sabbath gets its name from the first word of *Isaiah*, chapter forty, which is the section of the Prophets read in the synagogue on that day. The first two stanzas (quoted here in the American-Jewish translation) are particularly important in terms of *Dos Kleyne Mentshele*:

> Comfort ye, comfort ye My people,
> Saith your God.
> Bid Jerusalem take heart,
> And proclaim unto her,
> That her time of service is accomplished,
> That her guilt is paid off,
> That she has received of the Lord's hand
> Double for all her sins.

Abramovitsh's reference to this particular Sabbath serves several functions. First, by having his hero see Golda on this day, he underscores her essential goodness and the possible benefit that he could reap from her influence. Second, with all the castigation that the book contains and all the misery that it depicts, this reference would remind people of God's promise of comfort after a time of suffering and punishment and would help them in their struggle against the various evils they faced. And last, because the Torah reading for Sabbath Nachamu contains the Ten Commandments and the Shema (the section beginning "Hear O Israel, the Lord thy God, the Lord is one," the essential statement of Jewish belief), Abramovitsh's reference shows how far Yitzchok-Avrom was from true Judaism. The corrupt town leaders always tried to prove that their actions were in line with religious law, but their assertion was disproved by the source of that law, the Torah, as Abramovitsh makes clear. Thus, although Sabbath Nachamu seemed to be mentioned simply in passing, Abramovitsh used it to highlight the problems and struggles that were the central focus of his book.

But it is Abramovitsh's social commentary that is most important; and even his artistry was intended in part to raise the taste of his audience. The distress of the Eastern European Jewish community, caused by internal and external forces, was appalling; and Abramovitsh's work, so far as it concerned social and economic problems, was truly radical. What lay behind Mendele's popularity (and Abramovitsh's relative anonymity) was the way Abramovitsh used Mendele, one of the common people (as he presented himself in the preface to *Dos Kleyne Mentshele*), to speak for and to—rather than down to—the common people. He was not interested in simply attacking Hasidism or traditional Judaism, nor did he want merely to attract a small circle of Maskilim. Rather, he wanted to help his whole people, especially the poor and downtrodden among them, by showing them what lay behind their misery, by beginning to educate them, by making them aware that their lives could be improved, and by encouraging them to take action that would bring about this improvement. *Dos Kleyne Mentshele* was his first step in this endeavor. Its success, artistically and socially, made possible what was to follow.

CHAPTER 4

Di Takse *and* Di Klyatshe:
A Time to Kill and a Time to Heal

I *Mounting Anger*

*D*os *Kleyne Mentshele* was enormously popular even in its first version, and Abramovitsh filled the following years with a great deal of work. In 1865 he wrote the first version of *Dos Vintsh-fingerl*, and at the same time he worked on his book of natural history, the second volume appearing in 1866; and he transformed *Limdu Hetev* into *Ha'avot Vehabanim*. Of course, all during this time he was living in poverty and struggling to support his family. In 1869, his next major Yiddish work, *Di Takse, oder Di Bande Shtot Baley-Toyves (The Tax, or The Gang of Town Benefactors)*, appeared. This was the first of his two plays, though there is some doubt whether *Di Takse* was intended for actual stage production. The first real production of the play occurred in 1910 in Manchester, England, but Abramovitsh's son remembered less formal productions after the play first appeared in print.[1]

Di Takse is a strange work to discuss, because, while it was an important work in Abramovitsh's career, it is not nearly as good as his other major work. The work is seldom mentioned by critics and is almost never discussed in terms of literary craftsmanship, probably because it is one of his least artistic works. Significantly, it is the only one of his early Yiddish works that he neither revised nor translated into Hebrew. Although Abramovitsh's novels are characterized by their strong sense of drama and by an outstanding use of dialogue, his dramas themselves tend to be weak in these areas. In fact, whatever reputation Abramovitsh had as a dramatist was based on other people's dramatizations of his novels, not on his own works for the stage. There is, in *Di Takse*, practically no plot or characterization. The dialogue is often stilted, the action melodramatic and fragmented, the characters stereotyped. It is also, unlike his other satirical works, almost without humor. Whereas in *Dos Kleyne*

Mentshele we could laugh at some of the situations in which
Yitzchok-Avrom found himself or at some of his descriptions, at least
until the horror of his position became clear, almost nothing in *Di
Takse* provokes laughter. It is a bleak, bitter, despairing work,
closer to the primitive conception of satire as a curse than to modern
views of satire. As Dryden said, "there is still a vast difference
betwixt the slovenly butchering of a man, and the fineness of a
stroke that separates the head from the body, and leaves it standing
in its place."[2] *Di Takse*, unlike most of Abramovitsh's work, consists
of butchering rather than finely drawn satire.

And yet, though *Di Takse* may not be defensible on artistic
grounds, it is an important play. Its faults—and they are
numerous—are the result of zeal rather than any lack of ability, for
this is an angry work, a work filled with gall, with all the fury and
outrage Abramovitsh could muster. This is not the kind of Yiddish
work that is so often described by the phrase "laughter filled with
tears." It is a work of moral anger, behind which we can hear the
futile sobbing of the would-be reformer who feels himself helpless in
the face of overwhelming evil. Abramovitsh is not simply exposing
evil, revealing the reality beneath the appearance, as so many
satirists do—as he himself often did. He is not merely mocking the
evildoers, poking fun, ridiculing—he is reduced, out of frustration,
to calling them names.

Di Takse also represents the early stages of a revolution in Abramovitsh's conception of how the Jews could be helped. His earlier
emphasis on education as the Jews' salvation is here tempered by
the realization that education is not a practical alternative for people
who do not know that they need it in the first place. More importantly, education cannot satisfy hunger. One of the problems with
Di Takse is that Abramovitsh seems to be vacillating between the
educational principles of the Haskala and his own personal understanding of the situation. The resultant conflict, however, disappears in *Di Takse's* companion piece, *Di Klyatshe (The Nag)*, in
which Abramovitsh committed himself wholeheartedly to dealing
with the realities of the Jews' struggle rather than with the well-
meaning but perhaps misdirected ideas of the theoreticians.

II   *The Town Benefactors*

Because of its fragmentary nature, it is difficult to summarize the
plot of *Di Takse*. The basic outline of the play can be seen in the
descriptions preceding each of the five acts:

Act I: In which is shown how sixteen years ago in Glupsk there arose leaders, wardens of the tax.

Act II: In which is shown how the wardens will do anything to run the world.

Act III: In which is shown how several years later the people tried to depose the wardens.

Act IV: In which is shown how they collect the tax in today's world, even in 1870.

Act V: In which is shown all the things that take place with the new kind of tax collector. (11, 29, 45, 68, 88)[3]

The play focuses on the problems of the meat tax—how it is raised, how it is used by the rich leaders to increase their fortunes, and the effects of the tax on the poor people. With the exception of the hero, Vekker, none of the characters is very important as an individual, and all the conflicts between individual characters are somehow related to the tax.

Basic to the plot is an understanding of the tax itself. The play's title refers to the tax that was placed on two items: on candles, which were used for ritual purposes, and on kosher meat, meat slaughtered according to Jewish law and the only meat that observant Jews could eat. These taxes were imposed on the Jews as part of the Russian government's general anti-Semitic program, but Abramovitsh's protest was not yet against the Russian government. Instead he attacked the rich Jews who used the taxes for their own profits. This was made possible by the way the tax was collected: the government computed the amount of tax that it expected from every community and then leased the right to collect the tax to certain individuals, whose only responsibility was to give the government the specified sum of money. The tax collectors, however, also had to make a living, so that they tacked on whatever amount they thought they needed. For unscrupulous people this was obviously an opportunity to make a fortune: all they had to do was raise the tax and keep the surplus. In addition, after 1844, when the laws were changed, a certain percentage of the tax was supposed to be used for the maintenance of schools and other charitable functions; but again, unscrupulous tax collectors had no compunction about appropriating most of the money for their own use. *Di Takse,* then, is about the tax collectors; it is, like *Dos Kleyne Mentshele,* an examination of the internal problems of the Jewish people, ignoring, for the time being, the external causes of these problems.

The work opens with an introduction by Mendele Mocher

Seforim, who tells us that he received the following anonymous play in the mail, accompanied by a letter of explanation and a request that he publish the play so that all Jews would finally see the truth. Mendele, as he appears in *Di Takse*, is generally more sympathetic than he was in *Dos Kleyne Mentshele*, since he has learned the earlier book's lessons; and having been deeply touched by the play, he agrees to publish it, making only those changes that he feels are necessary. He begins by introducing his characters in a *dramatis personae* reminiscent of the one given by Axenfeld in his earlier play, *Der Ershter Yidisher Rekrut (The First Jewish Recruit)*. This consists of a list of the characters accompanied by editorial descriptions of them. Thus Mendele der Geller is described as "a smart aleck . . . who serves the benefactors and attacks whomever they tell him to"; and Isaac Zaikah is described as "one sacrificed because of his virtue" (9). As in *Dos Kleyne Mentshele*, the characters' names often have important meanings: Isaac Wolf Spaudik (Bothersome), Shemayah Tam (Simpleminded), Yossele Shinder (the Skinner), and the hero Shloyme Vekker (the Alarm Clock, or the Awakener). In addition, the *Dramatis personae* ends with the following cast of extras: "A poor Jew, a poor Jewess, aldermen, judges, slaughterers, women, geese, hens, turkeys, ducks, and a crowd of fifty thousand, which men shear like sheep" (9). The lack of subtlety throughout the *dramatis personae* (the sheep contrasted with Isaac *Wolf* Spaudik, for instance) foreshadows the bluntness of the play and indicates the angry, contemptuous tone that pervades the whole work.

The play itself describes how certain rich men, led by Spaudik, have become the tax wardens, ostensibly to protect the people from abuses but in reality to get as much money as they possibly can. These wardens are constantly complaining, either about what a hard time they live in (usually said at some kind of banquet, in front of a table laden with food) or about how ungrateful the poor people are after all that the rich have done for them. (As a number of the poorer characters say, they are on the verge of dying from such kindnesses.) In what amounts to a series of vignettes, we see how the wardens take advantage of the poor, circumvent government checks on their activity, take revenge on people who criticize them, and try to doublecross each other in their relentless pursuit of money and power. Interspersed with these scenes, we see pictures of poverty and protest among the poor, but the protest is overcome by the wardens' machinations and the natural fear that the poor have.

The closest we come to a developed plot is the part of the play concerning Schloyme Vekker. At the play's beginning, Vekker is presented as just another poor Jew whose only distinction lies in being better educated than most of the people. When we first see him, he is waiting to take dictation for Spaudik, because Spaudik, like Issar Varger, is practically illiterate and must conduct all written business through a secretary. While waiting, he reads a book of Yiddish poetry, an indication of how oblivious he is to the problems of the community. Soon, however, his friend Gedaliah Pikholz (Woodpecker), the rabbi of Tuneyadevka (Town of Idlers), enters; and in a lengthy conversation Pikholz informs the sublimely naive Vekker of all the abuses perpetrated by the rich. Furthermore, Pikholz announces that he has left Tuneyadevka because his protests have been ineffectual, both among the rich and the poor. No longer, he says, will he work on behalf of the Jews. From now on he will work only for himself. In a somewhat startling transformation, Vekker becomes a committed radical and in a significant gesture, rips up his book, explaining, in the language of Psalm 137:

> I am doing what our ancestors did—at the destruction of the Temple, by the rivers of Babylon. The musicians hung their instruments on the willows—they would no longer sing or play—they would only lament and mourn. Enough singing. Enough writing poetry, enough rhetoric when our people, our poor people sorrow by the shores of the Gnilopyatke. Rip the strings out of the Jewish fiddle. Jews were not born to sing, to play. We must be concerned with more serious things. Stay here, Gedaliah. We will try together to help our poor Jews. (26–27)

Unlike the biblical Gedaliah, who stayed in Judah as governor after the Babylonians destroyed the Temple and who was murdered by some of his Jewish subjects, Gedaliah Pikholz decides to go into exile. He will not let himself be murdered for supporting what he sees as a good Russian government against a corrupt Jewish one. Vekker, however, persisting in his naiveté, tries to enlist the wardens' help in bringing about reform, but he finally, after many years, sees the full scope of their corruption and, at great personal risk, appeals directly to the people. The people, though, are so afraid of the wardens that they turn on Vekker. Eventually, at the urging of Pikholz, who has returned as a government doctor, Vekker takes his family and flees from Glupsk. The final scene shows him on the road looking back to Glupsk and reflecting on all that has happened. Suddenly the sky is illuminated by lightning, which seems to go from the heavens directly down to Glupsk, and the play ends as Vekker says

Ah Glupsk! God's wrath has been let loose upon you. He afflicts you with His four terrible punishments. He punishes you with hunger; he punishes you with plague and pestilence, with cholera; he punishes you with fire; and he punishes you with wild animals, with town benefactors! God has punished you; He should have pity on you. He should make the good and merciful government looks on you with kindness and pity. They should correct the injustices, they should give you courage and protect you. They should bring order to you so that your crying, the moans of poor people, may no longer be heard. . . . You should serve as an example to all other towns. But for now, you're in a bad state, a very bad state. (120)

These recurrent references to the destruction of the Temple, the historic Gedaliah, and the potential good of the secular, non-Jewish government form a consistent pattern around the figure of Vekker, for whom a key concept is exile, diaspora, the scattering of the Jews throughout the world after the destruction of the Second Temple in 70 C.E. A common idea among the Maskilim, and one which Abramovitsh uses in *Di Takse,* is that hard as the exile may be, the Jews make it harder by not aligning themselves wholeheartedly with the governments of the nations in which they live. By keeping themselves so separated they have made themselves the object of persecution. This idea was expressed in the dictum to "Be a Jew at home and a German (or Russian or Pole) in public," a dictum that ignored both the nature of Judaism and the anti-Semitism that pervaded Europe and Russia. Abramovitsh is torn by the numerous contradictions he sees: certainly the Maskilim are right that the Jews have been too cut off from general society, and their isolation has allowed the Jewish villains to triumph by making the common people more afraid of the secular governments, however good they may be, than of the Jewish governments, however bad they may be. The isolation has also robbed the people of any awareness of their own power: the people could easily overthrow the Spaudiks and the Shinders if they would only stand up to them. On the one hand Pikholz says that the Jews "bring poverty and exile on themselves," while on the other hand he asks, "How are they guilty? What should they do, living in such dark times? . . . They have brains and feelings . . . they are humble and put up with a lot, but what does that help if they have no luck, if they've been stuck together for so many years in one place like sheep, so that they see no future before them and can't breathe free air. A man must eat . . ." (23–24). But who is to blame for this trouble? Vekker seems to have an answer: "Guilty are those circumstances, which have brought them to the point of having taxes. . . . Guilty are the circumstances, which have defeated them, which have made them fools and taken their courage. . . . But those circumstances have changed, with God's help, so stand up, Jews, rouse yourselves from your long sleep. . . . Be men with brains and courage, as God and our dear government have implored" (114).

Pikholz and Vekker, of course, represent a simplistic kind of Haskala idealism. Who, if not the government, created the ghettoes and the Pale of Settlement? And who made possible—even encouraged—the abuses of the meat tax? If the government had not imposed on the Jews a discriminatory meat tax, there would be no abuses. Furthermore, a Jew could not, in reality, decide to become a doctor and then receive the proper training as easily as Pikholz seems to. Certainly the corrupt Jewish leaders made things much worse but, well-intentioned though they are, Pikholz and Vekker respond with naive idealism. The Russian government had become more lenient under Alexander II, but past experience should have taught them that things would get worse again. What is especially sad is that the Jewish leadership had become so bad that the Russian government had come to seem a means of salvation. History would show that this appearance was illusory, but that it could even appear that way underlines the tragic extent of the breakdown in the Jewish world.

The plot, so far as it centers on Vekker, is unconvincing, which is too bad, because Vekker is basically so good. As Samuel Niger says, he is "the first social agitator in Yiddish literature."[4] He sympathizes with his people, he realizes that they are like innocent sheep being devoured by their wolfish leaders (an image that appears often in the play); and yet his progress from naive acceptance to naive reformatory zeal and then to self-imposed exile is too unnatural, contrived, and self-defeating. Of course he is discouraged and despairing, but it is simply out of character for him to walk out of the poor Jews of Glupsk and trust that the kindness of the Russian government will make things right. It was, after all, Vekker who said, "Cursed be he who sees such wrongs and is silent. Cursed be he who is a coward, who is afraid to speak the truth" (104). Vekker would not suddenly abandon the reality in favor of such a naive ideal, and the solution is no solution at all. Ultimately, then, the play is a failure, as Abramovitsh seemed to realize in never returning to it; however, it was an important step in his career.

If, however, the play is unsuccessful in dealing with the problems of Gedaliah—that is, the proper relationship between the Jews and the people under whose rule they live—it is successful in terms of showing the evil within the Jewish community; and this is what it is most famous for. The wardens' hypocritical machinations are exposed both in relation to cheating each other and, most importantly, to cheating the public. Thus Spaudik, who pretends to be a traditional religious Jew (we first see him studying Talmud), has no qualms about being allied with Standhaft, a Germanic, less observant Jew, as long as the coalition works to his own advantage. Matters of principle are never allowed to interfere with matters of profit. Spaudik, whose evil nature is apparent to us (for one thing, he has hemorrhoids), is constantly bewailing the fate of the Jews, even as he takes a leading part in creating that fate. His concern, like that of the other wardens, is evident the first time they gather to raise the tax. They are sitting at a feast, in front of a table laden with food.

MOSHE BAAL TACHLIS: It's not good business to take in only twenty-five kopeks for a piece of meat in times like these. It's enough that we busy ourselves with the tax for the good of the community. Why should we lose money on the deal?

TAM: Why should we lose money?

STANDHAFT: We're not obliged to lose money! Everybody should be eating meat and we should pay for it? Enough is enough, let's increase the shortage of meat.

REB JOSEPH: All right! We can increase it.

SPAUDIK (sighs): It's surely a pity for the poor, for the poor Jews, but what can we do? Surely God can help. But meanwhile it's no big thing to raise the tax a couple of kopeks on a piece of meat.

REB JOSEPH: Sure. What can it hurt?

TAM: Why not three kopeks?

STANDHAFT: Why not four? Is four too much? Should the town get less? Where would people get money when they needed it?

SPAUDIK (rolling his eyes and sighing): Surely our people's needs are great. Jews don't have very much. No. Let's raise it five kopeks. First of all, I don't like even numbers and second that'll make it a round thirty. (30).

The leaders' complete disregard for the people is overwhelming, as is Spaudik's constant expression of sympathy in the process of making things worse. Several times Spaudik indicates that he is willing to trust in God to save the poor while the rich wardens grow richer.

The wardens, then, have become like the tyrannical leaders of any other government. They have lost touch with the people whom they are supposed to protect and they regard the government as something that operates for their own benefit. Their independence from the people is shown numerous times. When, for example, the people have demanded an accounting of the tax funds, Tam exclaims: "Whose business is it what we do with the money? Who wants to mix in our affairs? We're the wardens!" (33); and a little later Spaudik poses the key question, a question reminiscent of *Dos Kleyne Mentshele*: "Who listens to the rabble rousers, the loafers, the common people? I ask you—who is the town? Is it us or the beggars, the workmen? Ha? Who is the town?" (51). Still later, as the leaders become even worse, even more willing to use physical force, Nathan Frechmann expresses total contempt for the Jews:

> Who listens to Jews when they protest? . . . They're like mosquitoes. They buzz around and think they make a terrible noise, but just wave your hand and they scatter to all sides. . . . They think they're clever, but they're the biggest fools in the world. . . . Try to set up a roadblock in Glupsk with a piece of rope and don't let people by unless they pay. Everybody will give you money, with nary a word of protest. . . . Or when there's a fire, everyone will come running, but not a single person will help bring water. . . . (83).

Of course his evaluation is right—the people are like sheep, easily led and ineffective; but their passivity is caused by having lived for so long under tyranny, both Russian and Jewish, and by sheer physical hunger. People who have to worry about where their next meal will come from have neither the time nor the strength to raise an effective protest. It is for this reason that Vekker must be unsuccessful in trying to rouse the people. His mistake lies in leaving rather than trying to understand why he has failed, for by leaving he gives the leaders exactly what they want—absolute domination.

Nor are the leaders afraid to use every means, including religion, to enslave the Jews. Thus, when they discuss what they should do with some extra money in the treasury, they decide not to build a hospital but to give each other interest-free loans, for according to

Jewish law, "This is one of the things on which no limit is set" (34). Of course they are technically correct, but they have totally distorted a law intended to benefit the poor by relieving them of interest payments. Furthermore, the leaders dictate religious law even to the religious authorities. They have, for instance, instructed the men in charge of deciding questions of *Kashrut* (that is, what is Kosher) to declare that large chickens are no longer kosher, causing more small chickens to be slaughtered and raising their income from the tax on slaughtering. And finally, following the methods that Yitzchok-Avrom described, they use the religion to put down dissent. When Vekker challenges their authority, they immediately charge him with being an *apikoros*, a heretic, an enemy of Judaism. As a result of this emotional denunciation, the people lose all sense of rationality and turn on him without considering the evidence. Vekker is discredited, though he is in no way a heretic. Thus even the religion, which sustained the Jews through so many centuries of torment, was taken over by the charlatans.

Di Takse, then, presents a rather bleak picture, with evil triumphing over good and the people condemned to live in the greatest misery. Here we come to the question of whether the play was intended for stage production. The editorialized *dramatis personae*, the numerous sarcastic stage directions, the footnotes by Mendele, the long introduction, and the stilted drama all give the impression that *Di Takse* is a closet drama. Ostensibly Mendele has simply published the anonymous play, having done just the slightest bit of editing; but as Miron has shown, Mendele's role is far more extensive. In a detailed analysis of Mendele's first paragraph, Miron demonstrates how Mendele's comparison of the river Gnilopyatke with the Nile and of the Mountains of Darkness with Glupsk are both comic and tragic in the juxtaposition of "biblical grandeur, remote and poetic, and ugliness and puniness close at hand. . . . This is his way of driving home—with a rhetorical shock—his idea of what present day Jewish life is like."[5] Furthermore, Mendele uses the wording of the Psalms to express these ideas: "Praised be the Creator, Who has created great oceans and many rivers. . . . Praised be His beloved Name for choosing us Jews, out of all the people of the world, to confer on us a Tax. . . . Praised be the Creator for everything He has created: praised be He for the wild animals, lions, leopards, wolves, bears, and for the tax-farmers. . . ."[6] Again, as Miron says, "The Psalmist praises God for

His infinite goodness. . . . Mendele insolently uses the same
rhythms to praise God for the brutality of an amoral Creation. . . ."[7]
Thus not only is the figure of Mendele distant from the author, he is
also distant from the mass of Jews for whom such words would
constitute blasphemy.

Mendele's cynicism, however, is different in *Di Takse* from what
it was in *Dos Kleyne Mentshele*. There he set himself up as superior
to the people until he learned his lesson from the rabbi's wife.
Having learned that lesson, he is now angry, outraged that Jewish
life must be lived under such hardship. Like Vekker, his eyes have
been opened, but this awakening brings more doubts and questions
than answers. Mendele's blasphemy appears to be not very different
from Vekker's, when he told a poor woman to use her last ten
groschen to buy a rope because "death is better than living to see
such calamities" (102). Mendele, however, discusses the problem of
such blasphemy in one of his footnotes. Commenting on Vekker's
surprise that people are silent in the face of injustice, he says that of
course the people complain among themselves in their homes but in
public appear to accept the injustices. One reason, he says, is that
they are so dispirited, but "in addition they are afraid to raise an
outcry against the evil men and publicize their falseness because
they know that the outside world blames the whole Jewish community for the infractions of individuals and attributes each person's sins
to all Jews. Hence it is better to suffer silently than to cry aloud, lest
the outcry emerge as blasphemy" (26 n.). Faced with the choice
between oppression at the hands of the Russians or at the hands of
the Jews, most Jews would choose the latter. In similar cir-
cumstance, the Hebrew novelist Peretz Smolenskin presented such
horrifying pictures of Jewish life that he insisted on modifying them
before he would allow his works to be translated into non-Jewish
languages, because, as David Patterson says, he did not want his
criticisms known "outside the family."[8] Thus, the mere fact that
Mendele protests against the injustices within the Jewish community could possibly be seen as blasphemy (Vekker, after all, is
treated like an apostate) and his more overt blasphemy in the introduction therefore becomes ironic. Many of the play's characters,
both good and bad, refer the community's problems to God; but as
the play indicates, the problems are human, not divine, and are
subject to human solutions. The problems as they are shown in the
play are caused by evil Jews in accord with the wishes of the Russian

government, and the real blasphemy lies in waiting for God to
rectify them rather than taking action immediately. Mendele's apparent blasphemy, even as he is taking action by publishing the
play, emphasizes the real blasphemy, part of which is exemplified
by Vekker's abandonment of Glupsk. Mendele stands in sharp contrast to Vekker: both find the situation intolerable, but Vekker
leaves while Mendele uses Vekker's failure to urge his readers on to
further action. This contrast between Mendele and Vekker, which
would be lost in a stage production of the play, is central to an
understanding of *Di Takse*, for Mendele (and through him, Abramovitsh) is taking a kind of action. Weighing the apparent blasphemy against the real blasphemy, he has taken the risk of publishing the play, of exposing the corruptions within the Jewish leadership in an attempt to do away with it.

Nevertheless, the work is seriously flawed. Miron rightly says
that it is "one of the most radical, shrill, and effective exposés of
social injustice within the Jewish community to be found in Yiddish
literature,"[9] but the solutions it offers (and while satire need not
offer solutions, *Di Takse* clearly tries to) are too hazy to be satisfactory. It is painful to have one's eyes opened to such cruel realities,
but Vekker's abandonment of Glupsk is self-defeating; and Mendele's publication of the play, while admirable, places too much
emphasis on the old standby of education, though as many of the
play's characters say, more than education is needed. Clearly
Abramovitsh was angry and in his anger vacillated between Haskala
theory and the physical realities. Already, however, in the softening
and changed direction of Mendele's cynicism, we can see
Abramovitsh working toward a new solution. As Niger says, if he
could not expect an uprising *of* the Jewish masses, he could more
consciously begin his battle *for* the Jewish masses.[10] This change
required him to abandon, even if only temporarily, his emphasis on
enlightenment, on the awakening that would prompt an uprising,
and to focus on providing the people with the basic necessities of
life. The seed of this transformation, evident in *Di Takse*, came to
flower in his next major Yiddish work, *Di Klyatshe*.

III   The Nag

Critics have speculated that Vekker was really a self-portrait of
Abramovitsh, a theory that is probably mistaken, for Vekker abandoned the battle at the same time that Abramovitsh intensified it. A

major difference between the two can be seen in Vekker's having voluntarily left Glupsk, whereas after the publication of *Di Takse*, Abramovitsh was forced to leave Berdichev. The play's depiction of the town leaders was so effective, so true, that the outraged officials of Berdichev made it impossible for Abramovitsh to stay. After considerable harassment, including threats on his life, Abramovitsh moved his family to Zhitomir, where he continued to live in great poverty. His plan for publishing a Yiddish newspaper never materialized, and, although in 1872 he received a rabbinical degree, he was unable to find a rabbinical job. (This is not surprising when we consider that the sermon he delivered in order to qualify for the rabbinate was a tirade about the meat tax, a subject not likely to endear him to the authorities.[11])

In spite of his problems—or perhaps because of them— Abramovitsh published in 1873 the first of his three greatest novels, *Di Klyatshe (The Nag)*. This work shows the extent of Abramovitsh's development over the course of a decade, moving from the idealism of *Ha'avot Vehabanim* to the relatively easy picaresque satire of *Dos Kleyne Mentshele*, through the bitterness of *Di Takse*, and into the sophisticated satire and imaginativeness of *Di Klyatshe*. Though Abramovitsh has often been compared to the great Russian satirist Gogol, and though *Di Takse* in some ways resembles *The Inspector General*, it totally lacks the wit and laughter of the Russian play. *Di Klyatshe*, on the other hand, owes a distinct debt to Gogol in its use of the grotesque, in its tone, and in its satiric outlook. It is somewhat like Gogol's short story "The Diary of a Madman," where the hero talks to, and is answered by, dogs: the hero of *Di Klyatshe*, Isrulik the Madman, holds lengthy discussions with the nag, a broken down old horse, and with assorted demons. Abramovitsh's work, however, has much wider implications than the Gogol story, and in overall effect is more like Gogol's novel *Dead Souls*, which surveys a large segment of society.[12]

These literary influences are certainly important, but even more important is Abramovitsh's account of why he wrote the work, as retold by Sholem Aleichem:

One summer day it happened that I was sitting at the inn in Glupsk, deep in thought, when I looked out the open window and saw an exhausted, sweaty Jew . . . who was standing there flogging a poor, tired, sweaty nag . . . which was hitched up to a wagon full of bricks. In addition he was

cursing—either at the nag or at himself or at the whole world . . . and the
nag turned her old battered chin toward him, looked at him . . . and, it
seemed to me that I heard her say:

"Fool! Call me a nag! You're a nag! Look around at this place and you'll
see that you're all nags—wasted-away, downtrodden nags—that sorrow is
the lot of all of you."

Thus I imagined the nag spoke; I raised my eyes to the place the nag had
indicated and I saw there a well-known Glupsk aristocrat [whom we have
already met so often]. . . . The fine man was standing with his hands by his
side, his hat at an angle; and around him milled the poorer Jews, like slaves,
looking at him like faithful hounds, rejoicing at his smile and trembling at
his scowl. And there came to my mind the verse from *The Song of Songs*

I have compared thee, O my love (O people of Israel)
To a steed in Pharaoh's chariots.

In this way I was prompted to give birth to *Di Klyatshe*.[13]

It is essential to understand that the parenthetical words in the
quotation are not from *The Song of Songs*, but instead represent the
rabbinical view that the love poem is an allegorical description of
the relationship between God and the Jews. According to this view,
the Shulammite woman who is addressed in this verse represents
the Jews; and it is this interpretation that Abramovitsh uses in making his nag—a far comedown from Pharaoh's fine steed—represent
his contemporary Jews.

Other influences on *Di Klyatshe* came from Abramovitsh's de-
veloping understanding of the Jewish situation. Whereas his earlier
work had dealt primarily with problems within the Jewish community, showing the opposition between the Jewish masses and their
leaders and containing a great ideal of Haskala criticism, *Di Klyatshe*
begins to concentrate on the whole Jewish people, seeing them as
victims of oppression from the outside world. As Niger says, *Di
Klyatshe* "may be regarded as the first manifestation of Jewish national consciousness in the new Yiddish literature."[14] There were
several reasons for this shift, but the main reasons concerned the
Haskala and the reign of Alexander II. As we saw in *Di Takse*,
Abramovitsh had already begun to question the goals and methods
of the Haskala; and he came to realize more and more that much of
what the Haskala was doing, admirable as it may have been, was
irrelevant to the real situation of the Jewish people. The Jews were,
in reaction, rejecting all facets of the Haskala. This criticism, as we
shall see, comes through very strongly in *Di Klyatshe*.

Behind this irrelevancy, however, lay a faulty understanding of the Russian government. Alexander I and especially Nicholas I had made the Jews' lives so miserable that the minor reforms of Alexander II seemed to herald the coming of the Messiah. His freeing of the serfs (coupled with reports of the freeing of the slaves in the United States) and his modification of some anti-Jewish laws led the people to believe that they would soon be freed of all restrictions and would be accepted as Russian citizens; but in the early 1860s, Alexander's chief advisers "were still adhering to the old doctrine that Jews should be granted equality only after they had proved their usefulness to the country."[15] Unfortunately, many of the Jewish leaders associated with the Haskala, with their belief in their people's backwardness, were willing to accept this kind of slow progress, and thereby encouraged discriminatory treatment of the Jews. Finally, after about 1863, all semblance of liberalism ended; and, symptomatically, in the late sixties and early seventies anti-Jewish riots took place in Odessa. The Jewish leadership, however, which had staked its reputation on the good will of the government, could not bring itself to recognize the new reality and continued to preach that the Jews must—and could—earn equality. By the time he wrote *Di Klyatshe*, Abramovitsh understood both what the government was doing and the flaws in the Haskala position; and it is these elements that form the background of his allegorical work and explain his move toward Jewish nationalism.

Di Klyatshe is a funnier and more subtly satiric work than anything Abramovitsh had yet written. It begins, of course, with an introduction by Mendele, who ironically praises God for having allowed his horse to die from hunger. This tragedy turns out not to have been all bad, because a friend offered to give him a new horse—that is, the manuscript of *Di Klyatshe*—which Mendele has edited and is now publishing. He concludes the introduction with a lesson on how to read the book.

The story itself is told by its hero, Isrulik the Madman, who is a staunch adherent of the Haskala. Isrulik, it seems, has refused to follow the usual pattern of Jewish life, which he describes as consisting of early marriage followed by terrible poverty. Instead, he wants to enter a Russian university and become a doctor, and, in spite of his mother's determination to marry him off, he spends all his time studying secular subjects, some of which even he thinks are silly, so that he may pass the entrance examination. However, all this study-

ing affects his health; and one day, while walking in the woods, he
loses consciousness and has a fantastic vision. First he sees a herd of
beautiful horses in a field, but soon he shifts his attention to a dismal
looking old nag who is being pursued by dogs and stone-throwing
children. Since Isrulik is a member of the Society for the Protection
of Animals, he feels compelled to intervene on the nag's behalf, and
though the children jeer at him, they eventually leave. Isrulik then
brings hay to the nag, who has meanwhile fallen into a mud hole,
and tries to console her, speaking a language which he calls "Horsish." To his surprise (and ours), the nag answers him in Hebrew and
then in Yiddish. This nag, it seems, is not really a horse but a prince
who has been transformed; and the nag's history is an allegorical
history of the Jews from the time of their slavery in Egypt, where
the prince was first transformed into a nag. During the course of
their conversation, Isrulik is alternately angry with and sympathetic
toward the nag; and while he thinks about the problem of
reincarnation—perhaps he is King Solomon or the Queen of Sheba
or Judah Maccabee reincarnate—a host of demons appear, one of
which rides off on the nag.

Suddenly, Isrulik wakes up and finds himself in his own bed,
surrounded by his mother, a Jewish wonderworker, and his non-
Jewish assistant. During the next few days, both his mother and one
of her employees chastise him for his irregular behavior: for his
attachment to secular books, and especially the storybooks, which
they blame for his strange vision; for his refusal to marry and settle
down; and for his rudeness to various town dignitaries. Nevertheless, he soon returns to his studies, goes to take the examination,
and fails because he is unable to answer an irrelevant question about
the Russian witch Baba Yaga. This failure affects his mind, and the
rest of the novel deals with his further visions concerning the nag
and Asmodeus, king of the demons.

The visions begin as he rescues the nag from two policemen who
are leading her out of town. In the woods he has a series of conversations with her, in which we again see his combined feelings of love
and contempt toward her, and he also has a series of dreams: he sees
himself enthroned in Paradise, then meets the demon Kashchei,
who summons wild beasts and transforms them into beautiful women. Isrulik then reads to the nag a letter he has sent on her behalf
to the Society for the Protection of Animals and the Society's response, and he again chastises her for her way of life, until a peasant

appears and frightens him; but he continues his harangue when the peasant has gone, only to be interrupted by Asmodeus, who teaches Isrulik a great deal about the ways of the world and takes him high into the heavens so that he can get a broader perspective of the earth; and when Asmodeus learns that a tax collector, one of his followers, has died, he tries to make Isrulik take his place. Isrulik almost obeys, until he learns that he must ride the nag. When he refuses, Amodeus, in his anger, hurls the poor boy through space, at which point Isrulik wakes up to find himself in bed surrounded by the same group as before. The book ends with the wonderworker blaming Isrulik's problems on demons.

Even this brief summary should indicate how different *Di Klyatshe* is from the earlier works. While Abramovitsh still deals with the terrible realities of Jewish life in Russia, he does so in a new way, largely without the realistic melodrama he had used before. He is closer here to Dryden's "stroke that separates the head from the body, and leaves it standing in its place." Partly this is the result of shifts in his satiric target and tone: his target is no longer the evil leaders of the Jewish community, but rather the anti-Semitic outside world and the foolishness of Haskala leaders; his tone is no longer one of pure condemnation, but has moved to the more effective level of ridicule. And all of this is conveyed by a fanciful and entertaining allegory.

The most important elements in the allegory are the nag and the Society for the Protection of Animals, which represent the Jewish people and the Haskala, respectively, while Isrulik represents the eager young Maskil who is filled with ideals but is devoid of experience. Abramovitsh had actually intended, in the early 1870s, to publish a series of works under the title *The Works of Isrulik the Madman*, but he never got very far with the project. The basic idea behind the project was that books were being written for everyone except the fools and the madmen, and Isrulik, being something of a madman himself, intended to make up for this omission. Abramovitsh used the old idea that the madman is in many ways more sane than his fellow men, so that Isrulik "sees clearly how really crazy is the world of the 'clear thinkers' "[16] Abramovitsh, however, did not get very far with this project (the most representative work, "So, Who's Crazy?" takes up four pages in *Mendele un Zayn Tzeit*), and the character of Isrulik in *Di Klyatshe* is much more complex than in the projected works.

The basic conflict that Isrulik faces is indicated even by his name, a Russianized version of "Israel," and in a number of significant spots he is addressed quite simply as "Israel." Poor Isrulik, unlike Vekker and Pikholz, finds that one does not become a doctor simply through desire—the Russian government is not quite so liberal as *Di Takse* had implied—and Isrulik's wish to be assimilated into Russian society, to combine his Jewish and Russian identities according to the Haskala's program, meets with many obstacles. His first obstacle is the traditional Jewish way of life, whose major spokesman in the book is his mother. Almost every time we see her she is appealing to him to marry and settle down, to give up his secular studies and return to the old ways; but Isrulik will not submit. He invariably directs her attention to what has happened to his childhood friends, who followed all the traditional customs. Now they are fathers, though still young, without professions, without education, living in great poverty. Such a life is not for him. " 'I am impelled to break my bonds and to live on the same footing with all men of the vast human race, to make every effort to improve my lot without en-croaching on my Jewish heritage. . . . My aim is merely to improve my lot through education (69–70)' "[17]. And his belief that he can help his people by becoming a doctor simply emphasizes his naive idealism.

Another obstacle is the course of study he must follow to pass the examination. "Mathematics, physics, Russian grammar, and even the dead languages were as easy to me as falling off a log. The only things that came hard were history and what the Russians called literature" (17). As he makes clear many times in his comments on the nag's history—the history of the Jews—history is not one of his best subjects. (In "So, Who's Crazy?" Isrulik says that the Jews "know almost nothing of their own history. Ask even the greatest scholar something about Jewish life . . . and he'll look at you as though he were asleep and he'll tell you how four thousand years ago they crossed the Red Sea, a little bit about Purim, a little about Chanukah, something from Spain, something from Chmielnicki's time, a touch here and a touch there and that's it. . . . But without history a people loses its value. . . .")[18] In *Di Klyatshe*, of course, his complaint is directed against world history, but how can he become a citizen of the modern world if he will not study history, even if it is only the story of "how often people all over the world, from the creation of the universe down to our own time, had been spoiling for a fight, had mauled and killed one another . . ." (18)? His attitude toward the literature he must study further emphasizes his almost schizophrenic relationship to the two worlds of Judaism and Russian life. On the one hand, he objects to having to study such mythological subjects as "werewolves, wood-demons, and witches, of Waters-of-Life and Waters-of-Death, of firebirds and golden apples," while on the other hand he defends them to his mother by saying, " 'Now, Mother dear . . . don't we come across just such stories in our Talmudic lore? Haven't you told me quite a few of them yourself?' " (18, 59). He may personally consider them a waste of time and a burden, but because they belong to the modern world to which he aspires, he insists on defending them. Jew? Russian? Russian-Jew? Isrulik has trouble making up his mind. He wants to belong to both worlds, though they are in so many ways irreconcilable and though, as he will learn, the Russians do not particularly want him.

But Isrulik is brimming over with Haskala idealism, just like the Maskilim who refused to acknowledge Russian anti-Semitism. He thinks that he has the solutions for all the nag's problems, that if she would only do what he says she would be accepted by society and be transformed back into a prince; and when the nag ignores his harangues in order that she may eat or simply wander around, his attitude quickly becomes that of the anti-Semite: "I regarded her as beyond all hope. . . . She would never amount to anything. There was evidently something in what her enemies said about her. The whole world could not be wrong. She was, assuredly, an ill-fated wretch, an outcast of society. Why should I keep watch over her and minister to her?" (140). Isrulik's words are indicative of the problem that Abramovitsh was examining, the tendency among many Maskilim to think they had all the solutions for improving the lot of the Jews within Russian society and their consequent tendency to turn against the Jews when the common people rejected those solutions, when the people decided they would rather have bread than education as a first step in their emancipation. Many of these Maskilim, like Pikholtz, decided that the Jews were beyond help, "would never amount to anything," and therefore abandoned the struggle rather than question their own biases. Herein lie the central questions of *Di Klyatshe:* what is—and what should be—the relationship between the educated, modernized, supposedly Russianized Maskilim and the great mass of Jews leading lives of poverty and isolation within the *shtetls?* Are the reformers' reforms practical? Will they work? If not, what do the people need? Isrulik, though often infuriated with the nag, has a good heart. His sympathy for her plight always manages to overshadow his anger with her; but many of the Maskilim were not so charitable, as can be seen in the correspondence between Isrulik and the Society for the Protection of Animals, which is itself a satiric representation of the Society for the Promotion of Haskala, an organization that was founded in December of 1863.[19]

Isrulik's letter on the nag's behalf, though naive and inane, is also humane. He begins by describing the 1870s as the Humane Era and then citing the Society as partial proof that he is right. Amidst a great deal of irrelevant verbiage, Isrulik finally calls the Society's attention to the nag, pointing out the injustices she has suffered, comparing her to the outcasts of Indian society and the recently freed slaves of America, and asking the Society to " 'intercede in her behalf. Give her your protection . . .' " (124). As the nag herself points out, much of the letter consists of two elements: *melitza*, the flowery, ornamental style of writing that so many of the Maskilim affected; and attempts to show off his knowledge; but basically the letter is idealistic and well-intentioned.

The Society's response, however, manifests the kind of arrogance that so often afflicted the Haskala. Their letter begins by bluntly, if accurately, telling Isrulik that his letter was hard to understand, but that they have received many letters about the nag. Some of their correspondents have agreed with Isrulik, but others

take a diametrically opposite view. "You cannot and should not clash with those who deal the animal an occasional blow, they instruct us. "Such severe treatment is imperative—one cannot do without it." According to those who hold this opinion, the animal's behavior is rather reckless and her appearance is freakish. When attempts are made to harness her, she balks and backs away. . . . She must be lashed now and then—there is no managing her without a whip. It would be absurd to keep her with other horses; she would prove highly contagious. And as far as work is concerned, she can hardly stir her stumps and is fit only for certain degrading tasks. . . .
. . . We must earnestly suggest that you pay no attention to her, and refrain from calling to task those who occasionally chastise her. Our men cannot commiserate with just any animal, indiscriminately. You need have no fear that the punishment she receives is undeserved. . . . (126–27)

Still, the Society has formed a commission to study the nag's situation, and if the first part of the letter is cruel, the part containing the commission's recommendations is worse:

> In its report the Committee recommends, first of all, that the nag . . . be made somewhat more presentable. Furthermore . . . it is felt that something ought to be done about her crass ignorance. For one thing, she ought to be trained to a proper gait, and so forth. Only then may she be considered entitled to our consideration. Only after she has acquired all the distinctive traits of a trained horse will our Society espouse her cause and see to it that she is not molested. In the meantime, every precaution must be taken to keep her out of the grain fields—primarily for her own good. (128)

The satire here is directed against those Maskilim, including, in a modified way, Isrulik and the young Abramovitsh, who believed that the Jewish people had to earn their basic human rights, their equality with other Russian peoples. This, in a far less arrogant and doctrinaire way, was also one of the lessons of *Dos Kleyne Mentshele*: become educated, learn a trade, so that the Russian people will accept you, so that you will be accepted in Russian society. Then your poverty and your hunger will disappear. By 1873, many Maskilim suspected that this idealistic plan was futile, though the most doctrinaire Maskilim would not admit their failure. Even Isrulik, who has been kept out of the Russian university because of the stiffer requirements that Jews had to meet, thinks that the Society's answer is reasonable, just as he had earlier condescended to speak "Horsish," a satiric jab at the Maskilic scorn for Yiddish, the language of the people they were supposed to be helping. Furthermore, as soon as Isrulik finishes reading the letter, he is frightened by a Russian peasant, whose cartload of wood is being drawn by an ass. When Isrulik intercedes on the ass's behalf, citing his membership in the Society, the peasant invites him to help pull the load. Of course Isrulik refuses—his forte, like that of the Society, is in letter writing, not in giving physical aid to the creatures he seeks to help. And when Isrulik again protests in the name of the Society, the peasant responds: " 'I'll break every bone in your body, you crazy fool! To the devil with all your Societies!' " (130), and he proceeds to whip him.

Thus the Maskilim, for all their fine talk, for all their arrogance
and idealism, are ineffectual. They are fine at writing sophisticated-
sounding letters discussing their ideals and bemoaning the lot of
their charges, but they are actually scornful toward the Jewish
masses and unable to change the attitudes of either the Russian
intellectuals or the Russian masses. All they can do is preach to the
nag—they cannot help her. Even after Isrulik has fled from the
peasant, he can bring himself to tell the nag: " 'If you'll be submissive and conform to the good behavior and the ways of well-brought
up horses, you shall, with God's help, do well' " (132). Rejected by
society himself, Isrulik still cites imitation and assimilation as the
means toward achieving basic human rights and demands that the
poor nag show her appreciation: "Was I not holding forth on matters
of enlightenment and culture? I was beside myself at the thought of
her evincing so little appreciation" (136). The Maskilim, frustrated
by Russian society, turned their wrath against the Jews: in this
"Humane Era," in this time of the freeing of the serfs, in this age of
liberalism, the Russians could not be at fault. The blame must lie
with the Jews. Their attitude was like Isrulik's: "How could any
creature sprawl out like that in a stinking puddle, as placidly as
could be, and lie there, without sensing, without grasping all the
horror of its situation? . . . Did this creature have even the least
hint of a sense of honor? Was this unfortunate capable of awareness,
in any degree, of the bitterness of her lot, her boundless ignominy
and degradation? No!" (36–37). This is hardly the attitude of a successful crusader for human rights and helps to explain, from the
standpoint of the 1870s, why the Haskala, whose goals were ultimately so admirable, had such a dismal reputation among the Jewish
masses.

Even the nag, whose general passivity Isrulik comments on, is
impelled to argue with him. At one point, Isrulik is angry with her,
but "Suddenly the nag sighed. . . . The nag's one sigh had brought
about a complete upheaval within me, and my thoughts were ir-
resistibly drawn to her anew . . ." (37–38). When he discovers,
however, that her sigh arose only from her hunger, he becomes
even angrier and launches into a vituperative speech, using the
same kinds of superficial observations that oppressors have always
used to justify their oppressions. The nag responds in simple words,
avoiding Isrulik's rhetorical style but making much more sense:
" 'It's easy enough for you to say biting things!' the nag answered,

with a toss of her head. 'But let somebody else try living as long as I
have in a horse's hide, let somebody else be the victim of so many
humiliations, persecutions, blows, and wrongs at the hands of every
passer-by—I'd like to see then whether he wouldn't forget completely how to talk, and wouldn't actually become a brute beast!' "
(39). And she goes on to say that, though Isrulik does not know it,
her situation is better now than it used to be, no thanks at all to the
Society for the Protection of Animals. She denies that she does any
more harm in the world than any other animal, and she defends her
positive contributions, citing the "lovely circumstances" that force
her to be concerned with food: " 'To observe etiquette in my position is, you will admit, hard, quite hard. Nor is there any use for me
to wait in line, for the simple reason that my turn will never come' "
(46).

The nag speaks for the great mass of Jews, who worked honestly,
to the best of their ability, only to be vilified as lazy, harmful,
destructive people who did not deserve the same human rights as
other people. Certainly the nag grasps "all the horror of its situation," certainly she has a "sense of honor" as well as an awareness of
her "boundless ignominy and degradation." But what can she do?
All other creatures conspire to perpetuate her situation, and even
her presumptive protectors revile her, while they themselves are
often in a similar situation. The only way they can enter Russian
society is by abandoning their Jewish roots. They may have begun,
like Isrulik, by saying that they only wanted to be faithful Jews while
entering the mainstream of secular culture, but the historical reality
consistently showed this to be an impossible dream. As pious Jews
in the early nineteenth century maintained, "education without
emancipation leads to conversion."[20] The outside world was willing
to admit the Jew only if he went all the way to conversion, and the
hint of freedom that accompanied secular learning often led to that
end, for the serious student could often pursue his studies only by
giving up Judaism.

In short, as the nag implies, the Haskala's program is exactly
backwards. The first step must be emancipation—education and a
more modern lifestyle will follow. The nag is fully justified in asking,
" 'what relationship . . . is there between fodder, between suste-
nance, and the need for an education? By what code of justice can
you deny food and the right to breathe freely to any living being
unless it be proficient in certain arts?' " (143–44). She does not

dismiss education or deny its importance, she only questions
whether it is the proper first step. As she tells Isrulik: " 'Now, you
may be in no position to provide the nag with costly harness, the
complete trappings and so on, which are required for the perfor-
mance of fancy tricks. But as far as fodder is concerned and the right
to breathe and move about freely—these are of vital importance to
her existence and you must attend well to her needs' " (145). And
time and again the nag emphasizes that she is not begging for anything, not looking for pity or mercy, she is demanding something
that belongs to her but which is denied her—the right to live. The
Jewish people needed the removal of certain restrictions—quotas,
meat taxes, discriminatory laws—so that they could provide for
themselves. Philosophy, poetry, and science, important as they may
be, are useless to starving people.

And how does Isrulik respond to this outburst? " 'All I can say is
that it's the devil speaking through your mouth today—none other
than the devil himself!' " (147). Earlier Isrulik had compared the
nag to Job because of their common suffering. Now Isrulik is playing
the part of Job's comforters, ignoring the realities that the nag points
out, seeking rationalistic explanations for her situation, and trying to
blame her for her own misfortunes. Like many people, when he lets
his feelings guide him he is helpful and compassionate, but he is
most dangerous when he rationalizes, when he lets himself be
guided by dogma. Isrulik is right in seeing a devil at work, but he is
wrong when he attributes the nag's outburst to demonic possession,
for we almost immediately meet Asmodeus, the prince of the demons.

Asmodeus is a strange kind of demon, not at all like the devil of
Christian theology. On the few occasions when he is mentioned in
the Talmud, for instance, he is never cited as an evil force. Instead,
he is responsible for preserving "the ethical order of the world."[21]
In addition, he is a trickster who thrives on illusion. The most
famous story about Asmodeus, a story alluded to in *Di Klyatshe*,
concerns the tradition that when King Solomon built the temple, he
used no iron tools to split the rocks. Instead he used the *shamir*, a
small worm that could cut its way through the hardest rocks; but in
order to get the *shamir*, he had to trick Asmodeus and take him
prisoner, since only Asmodeus knew where the *shamir* was. In return, Asmodeus once tricked Solomon into taking off the chains that
bound him and giving him the royal ring, one of the symbols of
kingship. Then Asmodeus picked up the king and hurled him four

hundred *parasangs*, about twelve hundred miles, after which Solomon wandered through the world until he could regain his kingdom.[22] In *Di Klyatshe*, Asmodeus helps put the discussions between Isrulik and the nag into a proper perspective by looking at mankind as a whole and then considering the plight of the Jews.

Early in his first speech—and Asmodeus is very fond of making boastful speeches—he tells Isrulik that " 'I, Asmodeus, do not corrupt the world as much as you, the humunculi, do. It's not so much the wickedness that you attribute to me which is responsible for all the misery and woe in the world as your own ingenuity' " (152).[23] He is not, at this point, thinking of a specifically Jewish problem. It is a problem in the nature of evil and is one of the facets of *Di Klyatshe* that adds to its greatness. Although it never loses sight of the specifically Jewish problems, it tries to put them into a broader context. The nag has already spoken about the relationship between the strong and the weak, about the rise and fall of the other horses, other nations. Now Asmodeus makes it clear that while he can point evil in whatever directions he chooses, the evil actually comes from within mankind. He does not corrupt ethics; he thrives on their corruption. Like a good satirist, he sees the hypocrisy that governs men's actions: " 'If truth and justice really predominated, you would never have developed such a taste for mercy and would not have so many merciful individuals, so many do-gooders, and so many humane societies' " (153). Isrulik's belief that he lives in the "Humane Era" is an illusion, and Asmodeus, like Abramovitsh, looks beneath the external appearances to reveal the underlying realities. That so many "humane societies" are needed indicates not that the world is humane but just the opposite. And the societies themselves offer no help, caught up as they are in theoretical concerns: " 'Here you are, confronted by a half-starved and completely broken-down nag, who is desperately in need of a little rest and a peck of oats or a handful of hay, but no—you go out of your way to show her how essential it is to master a few circus tricks' " (154-55).

As Asmodeus moves more directly to speaking about the Jews, he claims increasing responsibility for their problems, for he is still revenging himself on the descendants of King Solomon. As he tells Isrulik—and this is an important step from Abramovitsh's previous works—the Jews' problems would disappear if it were not for the persecution and torments inflicted on them by other people; but Asmodeus directs the evil that is inherent in people into anti-Semitism. Whereas Abramovitsh had earlier concentrated on inter-

nal problems, he now finds their real foundation in the outside
world: the tax collectors, the Spaudiks, the little men, the corrupt
religious officials, the arrogant Maskilim—all are the result of pressures brought to bear on the Jews by the outside world, under the
direction of Asmodeus; and the nag, the Jewish people, cannot be
blamed as Isrulik and Pikholz would blame them. On the other
hand, the Jews are not completely blameless either, as can be seen
in Asmodeus' curse on the nag: " 'Lend ear to all save your real
friends. . . . May you have knowledge of all things save the road that
leads to your happiness! . . . May your benevolent societies grow
rankle like nettles—and may their account books disappear without
a trace. May your taxes never cease. . . . And if someone ever intercedes in your behalf, may you fall upon him like madmen and
hurl stones at him' " (159). Certainly, as we have seen, this curse
had become the reality, but these problems are secondary, because
they result from the other, greater problem of anti-Semitism.
Spaudik is now seen as an effect, not a cause; and herein lies the
seed of Jewish nationalism: Abramovitsh seems to be saying, "Give
the people their rights and they will become part of modern society,
but do not condemn the people for the evils which have been imposed on them. Let the nag become a human being again; do not
condemn her for being a nag." Part of the greatness of *Di Klyatshe*
lies in the way in which Abramovitsh's observations have a universal
significance at the same time that they deal with specifically Jewish
problems.

Asmodeus, however, is not yet finished with Isrulik, for a short
while later Isrulik awakens from a faint to find himself sitting in
Asmodeus' hand while the demon flies through the sky. This section
of the novel is reminiscent of *The Dream of Scipio,* the last section
of Cicero's *De Re Publica*, in which Scipio is taken aloft by his
grandfather's ghost—in a dream, of course—so that he can look
down at the world and see things in their true perspective. Like
Scipio, the self-important Isrulik must have some of his illusions
shattered. First he sees a battlefield after a battle; mutilated corpses
lie everywhere, vultures and wild animals are devouring the flesh,
and men are looting the bodies. Isrulik, who thinks he lives in the
"Humane Era," who earlier had referred scornfully to the battles he
was forced to study in history, is horrified at how the reality
punctures the theory. As Asmodeus has implied, the world is still
savage, and for this reason, as well as others, Isrulik's theories are
bound to fail.

The next scene Isrulik sees looks at first like a riot in some strange city in Rumania. His sympathy aroused, Isrulik cries, " 'I hear screams, the outcries of unfortunate creatures. I can hear groaning and death rattles. . . . Let there be an end to wars, to brutality, to bloodshed!' " (171). Isrulik's universal sympathy is admirable, but his anguish increases when Asmodeus laughingly informs him that he is observing a pogrom, something that should surely be out of place during the "Humane Era." As Isrulik pleads that he be spared the view, Asmodeus again attacks his approach to history, for while the young Maskil is willing to mourn over historical persecutions, he refuses to acknowledge contemporary ones; while he is willing to weep at the nag's history, he refuses to comprehend her current position, because it contradicts his beliefs.

After these specifically Jewish references, Asmodeas shows Isrulik yet another scene of universal significance, a scene reminiscent of Dickens, especially the Dickens of *Hard Times*, which Abramovitsh might have read in translation. This is one of Abramovitsh's few comments on the nature of human civilization, and, true as it is, it seems almost out of place in his work. What Isrulik sees is a collection of factory smokestacks spewing out the filth that is a by-product of the manufacture of guns and cannon, of machines that will deprive people of work—in short, "the smoke of civilization" (180). He also sees a quiet pastoral scene and then the same scene after it has been destroyed by civilization. This is Asmodeus' realm, the realm where men devour each other. As he tells Isrulik:

You half-wit, all those smokestacks of the countless mills and foundries are altars upon which incense is burned in worship of me and to the glory of the golden calf, the gods of speculation, finance, and plain fraud. That incense benumbs the emotions and shrivels the heart, turning everything into merchandise—love, friendship, piety, faith, charity, and so on— merchandise of one sort or another. And, what's more, the same smoke also ousts by degrees Him whose name I dare not mention. He is being cramped for space, little by little, and He is retreating, withdrawing from the scene, and there is hope that in time the earth will revert to me and become solely mine. . . . (182)

Luckily for us mortals, Asmodeus, whose power seems unlimited, cannot mention God's name, just as he has earlier been thrown into confusion by the sound of angels singing God's praises. He is not so much in control as he would like Isrulik to think. If he managed

once to dethrone Solomon, he was in turn dethroned; and if the
world is becoming his altar, that, too, shall change. But in order to
bring about such changes, men must be aware of the realities, not
allow themselves to think that they live in a "Humane Era." Abramovitsh knew that the economic and political systems were too
selfish, too unjust to be relied on. If people—and specifically the
Jews—wanted their rights, wanted to be able to live like human
beings, they had to find some way other than appealing to the good
will of the government, for as Abramovitsh shows time and again,
the government had no good will. It was there to serve itself, and its
leader was Asmodeus, prince of demons.

After this Dickensian vision, the scene dissolves to a demonic
party, with dancing and drunkenness. Isrulik now sees more people
who are controlled by Asmodeus: first an anti-Semitic rabble-
rouser, a modern Haman, and then thousands of writers who work
for the demon. These turn out to be the Jewish journalists and
Maskilic writers who have been spreading Isrulik's kind of advice all
over the world. These writers are Asmodeus' servants to whom he
supplies pens, paper, and ink. As Isrulik watches them, he sees
several demons tormenting the nag by "ducking her several times in
the inky river until she came out jet black" (202). This is a visual
expression of what Abramovitsh has been saying: all the advice, all
the "enlightened" writing, has been a kind of torture for the nag,
without ever helping her. These are the people who have been
encouraging her to do "circus tricks" so that she may be fed, and
now we see that their inspiration (and Isrulik's) is demonic, their
work merely another form of Asmodeus' revenge on the Jewish
people.

Happily, *Di Klyatshe* is not so pessimistic as *Di Takse*, and the
novel's conclusion—like its numerous references to Isaiah, reminiscent of *Dos Kleyne Mentshele*—holds out some hope. Thinking that
he controls Isrulik, Asmodeus assumes that the boy will become one
of his "do-gooders," and though Isrulik protests at first, he is
frightened into accepting. After hearing Asmodeus' diabolical ten
commandments—actually, like Yitzchok-Avrom's confession, a way
to expose the sins of the public benefactors—Isrulik is dressed in the
clothing of a benefactor and the nag is brought in: "I gave way to
tears at the thought of having to ride her soon, of being a burden on
her back, but I could see no way out of my predicament" (213). That
is, Isrulik will add his own share to the nag's problems. As demons

tell him, " 'Blessed art thou in being privileged to ride such a nag—the world's nag' " (216). Everyone else, as we have seen has tormented the nag. Now it is Isrulik's turn, and though he apologizes to her—and feels sorry for himself—her burden will be no lighter. Finally, just as Isrulik, sitting on the nag, begins to comply with Asmodeus' demand that he swear obedience, he takes courage and refuses to continue. In spite of Asmodeus' wrath, Isrulik's emotional attachment to the nag has triumphed:

> My wretched nag sighed again—a sign of resignation which recalled to my mind all the sufferings and tribulations she had endured in her lifetime. Good heavens, I reflected, hadn't the poor creature suffered enough at the hands of others without my adding insult to her injuries? Let come what may, but I must not do such a thing. I must stand the acid test like a man of honor.
> "I will never take that oath!" I announced in a tone of finality. . . . (218)

Isrulik has committed himself to the nag's cause and has aroused the wrath of Asmodeus, but the virtue of his act becomes obvious when the demon picks him up and hurls him through space, for this was exactly the way Asmodeus had treated King Solomon. In fact, Isrulik's earlier reflections on whether his soul might have belonged to Solomon or to Judah Maccabee have, in a way, proved to be accurate. Like Solomon, he has deceived the demon in order to do something virtuous; and like Judah Maccabee, he has stood up for his people against a powerful opponent. Consequently, when he awakens from this vision, he is being embraced by his mother, that representative of traditional Jewish life. Of course, his mother is still very old-fashioned, but at least Isrulik knows where his allegiance should be, and he no longer thinks of her as the enemy.

But Abramovitsh, not one for easy answers, does not end the novel on this note. Rather, he ends it as the wonderworker blames everything that has happened to Isrulik on the demons. Whereas Isrulik's experience with the demons took place in a fanciful, imaginative, allegorical dream, the wonderworker refers to the demons as though they were a reality, thus reminding us just how much work the newly educated Isrulik has before him if he means to deal with people in a rational way.

Di Klyatshe is a fascinating, powerful allegory about the relationship between the Jews and the outside world as well as a commen-

tary on the role of the Haskala. This does not mean that Abramovitsh rejected the Haskala, but only that he was aware of some
of its excesses and failings and wanted to see them corrected. He
realized the importance of Jewish solidarity as an important step in
the attainment of true equality for his people, and he rejected the
implications that the Jews would be more quickly accepted if only
they were less Jewish. Nevertheless, even before Isrulik's ultimate
conversion, Abramovitsh allows him to show his real feelings for the
Jewish people in a beautiful monologue—one of the most poetic and
moving chapters Abramovitsh ever wrote. This monologue occupies
the eleventh chapter—"Isrulik Ponders on the World"—and concerns the scenes that Isrulik imagines as he listens to the plaintive
song of a nightingale, who makes even a cheerful song seem melancholy. This chapter contains not the brutal reality of *Di Takse* but a
more touching, pathetic view of the same situation. Isrulik's visions
concern a hen who has lost all her chicks (for some reason, this is
omitted in Spiegel's otherwise excellent translation); a Jewish
mother, who has lost her five sons to war, illness, pogroms, and
exile; a poor family ravaged by the demands of the community
leaders; and a group of "little men" at work. Near the beginning of
the monologue, Isrulik tells the nightingale that " 'it is the sad
interlude in your mellifluous chant that moves me most. For my
mother begot me amid stress and woe, she rocked me to sleep in
sorrow, and the song of affliction with which she lulled me to sleep,
has, alas, remained with me as my life-long song. . . . While others
bask in the sun I am destined to come to dark grief; while others
hold a jubilee out of doors, my back alley is plunged in mourning
over bloodshed, conflagrations, smoking ruins' " (98–99). Between
the visions, he returns to the nightingale, commenting on the song:
" 'Ease up a little nightingale—sing not so loud! Alas, one of my
heartstrings has snapped!' " (106). As in his earlier Yiddish works,
Abramovitsh focuses here on the misery and degradation of the
Jews, but there is more pathos and pity here than anger; and there is
also the kind of universal reflection that occurs often in the novel:
" 'You are wretched O man, because of your idle fancies. God
created man in His image, imbuing him with a human soul—the
same kind of soul for all men alike. You, however, strove to outsmart
the Lord's work and coupled this soul with another, a sort of folk
soul . . . and these folk souls are all too often antagonistic' " (107).

Altogether this is an exquisite chapter that can be read totally separated from the novel—an independent, delicate poem.

Di Klyatshe was the first of his Yiddish novels that Abramovitsh translated into Hebrew, and while the story remains the same, the tones of the two versions are very different. Abramovitsh's work in both languages was pioneering, but he was extremely sensitive to the differences between them. Whereas Yiddish was a folk language, a conversational and idiomatic language, Hebrew was a learned, formal one, a distinction obvious in the effects of the two versions. For example, chapters fifteen and sixteen in the Yiddish are entitled "Learn to Dance" and "Dancing Is no Substitute for Food"; the same chapters in the Hebrew version are entitled "A Sermon in Praise of the Haskala" and "What the World Exists on." The Yiddish is much more idiomatic in its equation of dancing with the Haskala program, while the Hebrew is less figurative.

Another difference between the two versions is a natural outgrowth of Hebrew's stature as the language of religion, for Abramovitsh, learned as he was in biblical literature, makes constant references to the Bible in Hebrew that were impossible in Yiddish. Thus, for example, when Isrulik's mother's employee chastises Isrulik, he concludes by citing one of Isrulik's more embarrassing antics, and he says, in the Yiddish version, " 'If the ground had opened before us, we would have jumped headlong into the yawning pit' " (65). In the Hebrew version, Abramovitsh incorporates a quotation from Numbers (16:32) that tells the story of Korach's being swallowed up by the earth: " 'We were ashamed of your words,' concluded Sender, 'and could only have rested if the earth opened her mouth and swallowed us alive at that hour. . . . ' "[24] Such references to the Bible add enormously to the sense of history in the novel and make it, in some ways, richer. On the other hand, Abramovitsh's Yiddish was so idiomatic and natural that the Hebrew seems slightly more distant from the problems that are so central to the novel. In short, both versions have their strong points, and part of Abramovitsh's genius was his ability to employ both languages to their fullest advantage.

Mendele's role in the novel is relatively small, but important. He begins by describing man as a microcosm who "combines in himself all species of creatures and creations." As Mendele describes this microcosm, however, he lists a significant selection of creatures:

"the lizard, the leech, the Spanish fly, the Prussian cockroach . . . a devil and a werewolf, a clown, a Jew-baiter . . . a polecat making its way into a hencoop and sinking its teeth into the necks of the poor little fowl . . . a monkey mimicking everyone in sight . . . a spider leading a fly astray, enmeshing it, strangling it, and sucking all the jucies out of it . . ." (9). Mendele has come to see the world as a hellish place, a place where men spend their time attacking and destroying each other; and when Mendele concludes his opening paragraph by saying "But that's beside the point," we know that this will be a central theme of the novel. And of course Mendele's description is borne out by Asmodeus, who shows Isrulik what the outside world is really like, thereby dissuading him from putting his trust in its good will.

Mendele also tells us that his horse died and that he subsequently came into possession of that other horse, *Di Klyatshe*; he follows this story with an explanation of the novel: "Each man will understand it in his own way and in keeping with his common sense. For honest folk who don't go grabbing at the stars in the sky, it will be simply a fairy tale. Those who look deeper may find in it a reflection of all of us who are sinners. Take me, now—I have seen in the nag all our little Jewish souls and have grasped the secret of why they exist in this world" (12). This is nothing more than a conventional description of the levels of allegory, in the tradition of Dante and Spenser—until Mendele adds his own interpretation and raises the question of "why they exist in this world." Although the answer is not entirely clear, it seems to make the nag a touchstone for the rest of the world, a reminder that man is not "humane," as Isrulik and so many other enlightened men would like to believe, and suggests that we live in a wolfish world where Asmodeus, operating through the free will that God gave to man, is the true ruler. Thus, if the Jews want their situation to improve, they will have to take their own initiative, not wait for the government or for anyone else. In this way *Di Klyatshe* is a true sequel to *Di Takse*, for it comments directly on some of the views expressed in the earlier work. Undoubtedly this is why the fictional rabbinical court in Glupsk released Mendele from his vow to publish a second part of *Di Takse*. By publishing *Di Klyatshe*, he has actually fulfilled his vow, and by even raising the question, Abramovitsh is forcing us to compare the two works. But whereas *Di Takse* is an angry and flawed work, *Di Klyatshe* is a coherent masterpiece.

CHAPTER 5

Masoes Bınyomin Hashlishi:
A Time to Break Down and a Time to Build Up

I   *The Jewish Don Quixote*

AFTER the strange world of *Di Klyatshe*, it is, at first glance, something of a relief to enter the apparently more humorous world described in *Masoes Binyomin Hashlishi* (*The Travels and Adventures of Benjamin the Third*). the second of Abramovitsh's great novels, published in 1878. This appearance, however, is misleading, for behind the humor lie the same problems and criticisms that had concerned Abramovitsh earlier; and the humor only makes his satire more effective. Nevertheless, even so perceptive and sympathetic a critic as Niger has written that *Benjamin the Third* is "an artistic parody in which the 'grandfather' abandoned sharp satire in favor of mild humor."[1] It is most important that the work's considerable humor not blind the reader to what Abramovitsh was really doing in this brief novel.

That the book is somehow related to Cervantes' *Don Quixote* strikes the reader immediately, but the nature of this relationship raises some questions. Niger, for instance, says that the book "is a parody of *Don Quixote*, not an imitation"[2]; but while he does point out many differences between the Spanish don and his Jewish counterpart, his argument is not very convincing and minimizes the importance of the work. In fact, *Benjamin the Third* belongs to that body of work that Paulson calls "the Cervantean anti-romance" and it functions in much the same way as its great Spanish forebear. As Paulson notes, "The Quixote syndrome . . . says that Quixote is totally wrong, that he is mad and the world is totally real; and yet he is right and the world is unreal or at least wicked and unimportant."[3] *Don Quixote*, that is, presents a double-edged satire: the fantastic,

87

idealistic hero is indeed a madman, out of touch with the times, dangerous, and laughable; at the same time, his idealism is laudable, for he only desires to help those less fortunate than himself, and the object of satire becomes all of the people he meets who mock that idealism. "If Quixote is a dangerously deluded fool, the people he meets are as dangerously *un*deluded," says Paulson[4]; and in fact the two edges of the satire are quite different. That directed at the don is primarily in the Horatian tradition, in which the satirist laughs at folly. That directed at his tormentors is primarily in the Juvenalian tradition, in which the satirist rails at knavery. Clearly *Don Quixote* is as much a lament over the death of idealism as it is a comedy about the don's peculiar kind of idealism. And although Abramovitsh, like all great writers, manipulated for his own purposes the conventions in which he was working, there can be no doubt that *Benjamin the Third* is a serious satiric work, one member of that large family of such works spawned by Cervantes' romance.

The plot of *Benjamin the Third* is actually fairly simple. In keeping with its nature as a Quixotic fiction, its plot is loose and episodic, describing the reasons for Benjamin's quest and the various adventures he undergoes in trying to fulfill that quest. The book opens with a brilliant, ironic prologue by Mendele, who simply cannot find enough ways to praise the hero of his book, the great world traveler, Benjamin of Tuneyadevka (Droneville), otherwise known as Benjamin the Third, who is a worthy successor to Benjamin the First, Benjamin of Tudela, the Spanish Jew who, in the thirteenth century, traveled extensively and recorded his observations in a well-known Hebrew travelogue, and to Benjamin the Second, Joseph Israel Benjamin, a midnineteenth century traveler. According to Mendele, the adventures of Benjamin the Third have been recorded in all the English and German newspapers: he has become a world celebrity, the recipient of a medal from the geographical society, and, all in all, someone of whom the Jewish people can be proud. Consequently, Mendele has set himself the task of delving "into the great treasure-trove of Benjamin's travels, available in all foreign languages," and giving a brief account of them "in plain, everyday Yiddish" (11).[5]

Mendele's account of the adventures, as Miron has shown, is a brilliant rhetorical tour de force, but the story itself is relatively straightforward. In the remote town of Tuneyadevka, an isolated town composed of poor Jews, one man, Benjamin, has immersed himself in the study of various travel books, like those of the two earlier Benjamins. Like Don Quixote, he gradually becomes obsessed by what he has read, and especially by various accounts of the legendary Red Jews, who live beyond the Mountains of Darkness on the other side of the river Sambatyon. These Red Jews are supposedly the Ten Lost Tribes of Israel, the Jews who were sent into exile when the Assyrians conquered their land in 721 B.C.E., and Benjamin devotes himself to finding them, so that all the Jews in the world may be united. Although Benjamin is "by nature, an egregious coward" (23), he puts himself through a peculiar kind of training and finally decides he is ready to go. With his own Sancho Panza, another poor Jew named Senderel, he sets out, determined not to be stopped by anything, not even by the Sambatyon, the legendary river that, for six days a week, rages so fiercely that it is uncrossable, but becomes a placid body of water for the Sabbath. The rest of the novel describes their travels through the towns of Pievki, Teterevka, and Glupsk, all the while satirizing both the travelers and the people they encounter. Finally Benjamin and Senderel are tricked by a pair of unscrupulous Jews and are forced into the Russian army, where they suffer grievously, until they are discharged for incompetence; and the book ends as they resume their journey.

There is some question as to whether or not the novel is complete, since the ending is rather abrupt, but this kind of ending often characterizes the Quixotic fiction, and it should be remembered that even the original version of *Don Quixote* did not bring the story full circle. It is entirely possible that Abramovitsh intended at some point to continue the story and just never got around to it, as Moshe Spiegel says in his introduction to the novel; but, although we may wish that Abramovitsh had written more, the final sense of the book is not one of incompleteness. Mendele often quotes Benjamin's own words about his journey, leading us to believe that he somehow finished the trip, but as Ruth Wisse shows, there was really nothing Abramovitsh could do but end the book at this point, for reasons that will become clear as we progress.[6]

II *Paralysis*

In the Yiddish works we have examined thus far, we have seen Abramovitsh alternating between realism and caricature. In *Dos Kleyne Mentshele*, for instance, Yitzchok-Avrom and Golda are three dimensional, realistic people, people we can imagine as having actually lived, whereas characters like the town leaders, Issar Varger, Dr. Steinharz, and even Gutman are types, caricatures, representatives of the forces of good and evil. In *Di Takse*, in spite of some human, affecting scenes, almost all the characters are types, with the possible exception of Vekker; and in the dream world of *Di Klyatshe*, only Isrulik is a fully rounded character (though in all three works, according to the requirements of satire, there is a strong pretense at realism, and in *Di Klyatshe* many of the things that Isrulik sees are reminiscent of Dickensian realism). Finally, in *Benjamin the Third* there are no real people: the characters are all caricatures, not simply and consciously evil like the characters in *Dos Kleyne Mentshele* and *Di Takse*, but caricatures in a more complex way. Perhaps the best example comes early in the book, when Mendele is describing the Jews of Tuneyadevka, whom he calls "a merry lot of poverty-stricken, devil-may-care optimists" in spite of their being "dreadfully poor":

Just ask a Tuneyadevka Jew (do it suddenly, however): "How do you get along?" He'll seem flustered, not knowing what answer to make at first, but on regaining his composure he'll answer you in all seriousness: "How do I get along, you ask? Ours is a kind Lord, I'm telling you, Who never forsakes His creatures! He supplies their needs and, I'm telling you, He'll go on supplying them!"
"Yes, but just what do you do for a living? Have you a trade of any kind, maybe, or a little business?"
"Praised be the blessed Name! I have—praised be the Lord—I have, sure as you see me, a gift from the Almighty—a musical voice. So, I'm the cantor during the High Holiday services in the settlements hereabouts. Now and then I perform circumcisions, and when it comes to perforating matzahs with the indented wheel, there's nobody like me. I also have a bit of luck once in a while as a marriage broker. I have a seat, as sure as you see me, in the synagogue. Then, too—just between you and me—I run a still that gives a little panther milk; I've also got a nanny goat—may she be spared the Evil Eye!—that's a good milker, and a well-to-do relative, not far from here, who likewise can be milked a little, whenever I'm really hard up. Aside from all these things, God is our father, I'm telling you, while the Israelites themselves are merciful and the sons of the merciful!" (17–18)

Like any good caricature, this one emphasizes certain outstanding traits of its subject, most prominently the absolute faith in God despite the horror of Jewish life in Eastern Europe and a deep-seated belief in the brotherhood of all Jews. No fewer than five times in this short passage does the speaker refer to God in thanksgiving, though the man obviously lives in almost absolute poverty. Furthermore, having read Abramovitsh's other works, we cannot completely share his faith in the unity of the Jews.

This short speech, however, states one of the major themes of the book. Abramovitsh, himself a religious Jew, would hardly satirize a belief in God (though Mendele often hints at such satire), and he at least hoped that the Jews might become unified. The problem that he exposes in this speech—and in the whole book—is one of paralysis. For the first time in his writings, the Jewish masses do not form the background against which the Yitzchok-Avroms, the Vek-kers, the Isruliks—villains, heroes, and Maskilim—play their parts. Rather, Abramovitsh focuses his attention squarely on the uneducated, downtrodden masses and finds them afflicted with an inability to act, to move, or even to feel the full extent of their desperation. God will provide, they believe, either through direct providence or by using another Jew as an intermediary. And if this is the case, they need take no action. There is paralysis everywhere in the book: in the fact that Benjamin's quest is so blatantly futile and foolish, and in the contrasting fact that he is the only character in the book who takes any action at all, however foolish it may be. Thus, he is certainly a *schlemiel*, as Ruth Wisse says, but in a strange, Cervantean way, he transcends that state.[7] Abramovitsh satirizes both Benjamin, the fantastic foolish dreamer, and the Jews he meets, who, whether they believe in his cause or not, find him a person worthy of serious consideration.

The sense of paralysis is obvious from the very beginning of the book, even in Mendele's ironic introduction:

Praised be the Creator Who fixes the destiny of the heavenly spheres and the fate of all His earthly creatures. Even the least blade of grass will not sprout unless some angel urge it on: "Grow, now! Come forth!" How much more so in the case of man, whom an angel most certainly must urge on: "Grow on! Come forth!" And still more with our praiseworthy little Jews. Among us no oaf dare open his mouth out of turn, a simpleton doesn't step into a sage's shoes, an ignoramus into a pietist's, a boor into a learned gentleman's, until such time as each oaf, simpleton, ignoramus and boor is goaded and urged on by some angel. It is likewise the angels who urge on our paupers of every sort, admonishing them: "Grow, ye poor, ye

beggars—beggars born, beggars broken-down, plain-spoken and close-mouthed—sprout, spring up like grass, like nettles! Go ye forth, ye Jewish children—go ye begging from door to door!"
But that's not what I'm leading up to. (9)

There is Mendele's old signpost again, and we immediately understand that this is exactly what he is leading up to, the idea that even the beggars are operating at a divine command, and that, consequently, salvation must come from some external source, that the people are waiting for someone or something to save them, but while they wait, they suffer.

Among the novel's major symbols for this kind of paralysis are the prayer house and the bath house. Ideally, the prayer house was a place for prayer and for studying holy books, and it was the common—and accepted—practice for wives to provide an income for their families while the husbands devoted themselves to study. In Tuneyadevka, however, as in much of nineteenth century Eastern Europe, this practice had degenerated. The wives, of course, still worked, but study was replaced by discussions of "family squabbles, political problems of Stambul, Turkey, and Austria, finance, Rothschild's fortune . . . rumors about government decrees, the legends of the Red Jews and so on" (16). There are lengthy discussions about these largely extraneous matters, questions of far-off politics and legends, but the men, who can fairly be described as idlers, do nothing about their own desperate situation. They are experts about the Turkish sultan or, later on, about Queen Victoria, but they are absolutely helpless in the face of their own problems. As Mendele says, they stay in the prayer house day and night, "praiseworthily sacrificing not only their own interests but those of their families to the public weal, wholeheartedly devoting their attention to these public affairs . . ." (16).[8] Often these same discussions are simply transferred to the bath house. In short, these people, believing that they are equal to dealing with the world's great problems, are paralyzed, oblivious to the problems that confront them every day, and, as a result, unjust to their wives, their families, and themselves. That Benjamin could rouse himself to any action in the face of such paralysis is almost commendable. The tragedy is that he is as misguided as the young Isrulik, for while Isrulik placed all his faith in the Haskala, Benjamin places all his faith in his own enlightenment, his own scheme for the salvation of the Jews; he is, in fact, a caricature of the Maskil who is convinced that he knows what should be done, but whose plans turn out to be fanciful dreaming, and who continues to operate in a state of paralysis.

The paralysis afflicting the Jews and their leaders is obvious in numerous other episodes. Thus, early in their journey, Benjamin and Senderel become hungry. Benjamin, in a characteristic action, begins to pray so that he may forget his hunger pangs; but Senderel reaches into his pack and pulls out a whole assortment of foods, to which Benjamin can only reply, " 'It is God Who has sent me this Senderel . . . even as He sent manna to the children of Israel in the desert' " (54). Benjamin's ideals, like Isrulik's, are entirely divorced from reality, from practical matters; and when he sees that Senderel has done something practical, he does not recognize his own impracticality but rather, like the typical resident of Tuneyadevka, he thanks God. He cannot understand that the people, himself included, must help themselves. Instead he relies on outside help, on God's direct intervention in his affairs; and while there might possibly be some religious grounds for such an outlook, to a reformer like Abramovitsh this attitude can only lead to paralysis.

In addition, this attitude can also undercut the religion itself. The best example of this comes late in the novel, when Benjamin explains that " 'we ought to close our eyes and place our trust in God, in the hope that come what may, He will bid His angels to guard us from evil. Could one, for instance, ask for better precautions than I bestowed on the bag holding my prayer shawl and phylacteries when I deposited it on a shelf right in the synagogue? And yet . . . when the Almighty refused to keep an eye on it, stolen from me it was, along with the rest of my belongings' " (94–95). If one relies entirely on the Almighty and refuses to be responsible for any action himself, then anything that goes wrong will be blamed on the Almighty. God "refused to keep an eye on it," says Benjamin; and the implication is that if the Jews are suffering, it is because God refuses to keep an eye on them, not because they wallow in inaction. In addition, Benjamin's reference to the angels who should "guard us from evil" recalls Mendele's reference in his introduction to the angels who are responsible for the growth and development of Jewish beggars. In short, Abramovitsh here presents the opposite side of the problem that we saw in *Di Klyatshe*. There Isrulik, the Maskil, believed that if the Jews would only take some action to improve themselves, they would be accepted by the outside world and their misery would cease. But here, inaction is a virtue, and action is not only undesirable but nearly impossible. As we saw, Isrulik's belief was untenable and inhumane. The beliefs of the characters in *Benjamin the Third*, on the other hand, are completely paralyzing, and what is needed is some kind of compromise between the Isruliks, the Maskilim, and the common people, between the daily struggle for bread and the ideals of the Haskala. It is not enough simply to wait for help, for the result is what happens when Benjamin, attempting to make himself less of a coward, finds himself lost in the woods. Because he is afraid of demons and monsters, he stays out in the rain, hungry, unable to move, and drenched. All he can do is pray until, as Mendele says, "Day, with God's help, broke at last" (27), as though the beginning of a new day came as a direct response to Benjamin's prayer. Helpless in the face of his own ignorance and cowardice, he can only pray for outside help and then regard the natural course of events as something miraculous.

Another example of the paralysis afflicting the Tuneyadevka Jews comes early in the book, when Mendele describes what happened when someone brought a date into the town:

How the townfolk flocked to gape at it! On opening the Pentateuch some-one discovered that dates were referred to in the Holy Writ! Think of it! Dates grew in the Land of Israel, actually! As they contemplated the date, a vision of the Holy Land spread out before them; here one crossed the Jordan; there was the Cave of Machpelah, wherein the patriarchs and the matriarchs are entombed, and the grave of our Mother Rachel; over there was the Wailing Wall; some bathed in the hot springs of Tiberias; others scaled the heights of the Mount of Olives; others still ate their fill of carob pods and dates, and stuffed their pockets with the sacred soil, ultimately to be placed in pillows under their heads in their graves. (19).

Of course the return to Israel had been, for almost two thousand years, one of the great dreams of the Jewish people, with its implications of universal harmony and the coming of the Messiah; and Mendele's picture accurately reflects this dream. But Mendele, not content to let this dream stand unchallenged, immediately contrasts it with another picture, a picture of the realities facing the Jews in Tuneyadevka: "The town's newly appointed Chief of Police ruled it with an iron hand: he had snatched the skullcaps off several Jews, cut an earlock from another, locked up several townsmen overnight for not having their passports with them; while from still another he had confiscated a goat merely because the animal had eaten all the straw from a neighbor's newly thatched roof" (19). There are two ways of regarding this juxtaposition. On the one hand we can say, "In the face of such anti-Semitic persecution, no wonder they dreamed of the return to Israel." On the other hand, we can ask, "Why, in the face of such problems, did the people dream of Israel instead of taking some kind of action to make their present lives better?"

It is worth remembering, at this point, that when *Benjamin the Third* was written, political Zionism had not yet been born; and although Abramovitsh was later to show some support for political Zionism (though he was never really a Zionist), in 1878 the dreams of the Tuneyadevkars are simply that: dreams. Certainly, considering their plight, there was justification for these dreams: Zionism, the people's desire for a land of their own, was a legitimate response to the anti-Semitic racism that pervaded Eastern European life, and escape from the horrors was clearly desirable. But their dreams had the result of precluding action, of shifting responsibility from the people to God and His Messiah, so that, like Benjamin, the people would stand and pray without trying to find their way out of the woods and then regard the coming of day as a miracle. (Even in 1909 Abramovitsh's practicality regarding Palestine was obvious in his response to a card he received from his friends Bialik and Ravnitzki, who were traveling in the Holy Land. The card showed a group of poor, ragged Yemenite Jews and bore the legend, "Another chapter from *The Beggar Book*," the Hebrew name of *Fishke der Krumer*. Abramovitsh, according to Joseph Klozner, was outraged: " 'What do they send me from the land of Israel? Do I have too few beggars, do I lack poor people here in the Diaspora? . . . And certainly there are others there—farmers, workers, many who use their muscles. . . . And they go and send me beggars—I don't have enough beggars here in the Diaspora?' "[9]) Dreams of Palestine or Israel are fine, if they result in action, in actual attempts at realization, but the dreams of the Tuneyadevkars constitute simple escapism, another way of not dealing with their problems. The sense of pathos that Abramovitsh conveys to us by juxtaposing these pictures lies in the fact that both ways of regarding it are correct. The dreams are entirely understandable and beautiful, and yet the inaction, the paralysis, is tragic. Unfortunately, the only action we ever see is

Benjamin's, action so deeply rooted in fantastical dreams as to constitute no action at all. Equally unfortunate is the fact that many of
the Jews regard Benjamin as something of a hero. Thus, when he
returns home from being lost in the woods, he is in a particularly
absurd situation. Tired, cold, and hungry, he has been lucky enough
to meet an old Russian farmer who is driving a cart full of produce to
a market town. Overcome by fear and fatigue, Benjamin faints, and,
when he awakens, he finds himself lying on the cart next to a trussed
rooster, who scratches him with its claws. Benjamin, of course,
immediately romanticizes his situation, imagining that he has been
kidnapped by a Turk and carried off into slavery. " 'If he would sell
me to a Jew, at least,' the wretched Benjamin mused, 'there may be
some chance of deliverance. But what if he sells me to some Pasha
or, God forbid, to some Pasha's daughters? In that case I'm lost—
lost forever!' And at that very point the story of Joseph and Zulenka,
Potiphar's wife, flashed through his head . . ." (30). His fear and his
imagination have combined to present a comic, yet tragic, picture in
which the beautiful and powerful story of Joseph is reduced to the
level of this poor bedraggled Jew traveling on a cart like a trussed
rooster. In Tuneyadevka, however, where Benjamin's disappearance has caused a certain amount of hysteria, his reappearance becomes a cause for celebration. Discovered with the potatoes, onions, and, of course, the rooster, Benjamin is immediately and
spontaneously hailed as a hero and led in a triumphal procession
through the streets of the town. No one recognizes the absurdity of
all that has happened. The mere fact that Benjamin has wandered
out of the confines of Tuneyadevka is enough to make him appear
heroic.

Lest we think, however, that this paralysis is confined to a little
town like Tuneyadevka, we also get detailed views of two bigger
cities. The first of these is Teterevka, "the first sizable city that our
wanderers had ever seen" (63–64). At first we may be inclined to
think that Abramovitsh is using the age-old contrast between the
city and the country to show the advantages of one at the expense of
the other. Indeed, Benjamin and Senderel do seem to be country
bumpkins adrift in the big city, overwhelmed by buildings of more
than a story or two, amazed by paved sidewalks when even the
floors in their own homes are not paved, bewildered by the constant
flow of traffic. At one point they are almost run down by a coach and,
in their hurry to get out of the way, they overturn a market woman's

basket of eggs. Finally, we think, we have left behind the paralysis of Tuneyadevka. Our expectations are dashed, however, as soon as Mendele brings us into "one of Teterevka's humble synagogues" (68), where the main subject under discussion is the Crimean War. Here the disputants divide into two major cliques: those favoring the British, led by Heikel the Philosopher, and those favoring the Russians, led by Itzik the Hairsplitter. Immediately we realize that the prayer house in Teterevka is just like that in Tuneyadevka, both filled with long, involved discussions of basically irrelevant matters. But whereas in Tuneyadevka some of Benjamin's cronies proclaim that he is "daft—he has a screw loose" (24), in Teterevka there is a detailed discussion of Benjamin's plans, with each side citing ancient sources and even the experiences of Alexander the Great to determine whether or not Benjamin has any chance for success. And one of Benjamin's supporters, Shmulik the Carob Pod, finally invokes, as proof of Benjamin's superiority, his "very absent-mindedness, his indifference, his wandering gaze, and his peculiar behavior in general . . ." (73). As Tevyeh Mak, another supporter says, " 'It looks to me as if Benjamin is on the right track, which may yet lead to the deliverance of the Jews from their Exile—' " (72). In short, these residents of Teterevka are, if anything, more ridiculous than their counterparts in Tuneyadevka.

On the other hand, and here is where the subtlety of the Quixotic fiction becomes apparent, some residents of Teterevka regard Benjamin differently. As Benjamin puts it, " 'They always welcomed me cordially and seemed to derive a strange joy from my presence. It was quite evident that they were extraordinarily pleased with me. I wish, from the bottom of my heart, that God and man may be just as pleased with them. Amen!' " (80). If the men in the synagogue are fools for taking Benjamin seriously, these others are knaves for making a fool out of him; and their knavery is further emphasized by Benjamin's wholehearted good wishes for them. Benjamin, however foolish he may be, is a well-intentioned fool, whereas these supposedly sophisticated people find him an object of humor, although they have no aspirations and no charitable feelings of their own.

In addition, Teterevka is a cruel place. " 'If, for instance, someone falls in the street, no one will lift him up . . . even if he might suffer a violent death there. . . . There are also some there who speak the language of thieves.' "[10] Benjamin's conclusion about Teterevka is that " 'it is no more than a kind of Tuneyadevka on a

larger scale'" (81). Benjamin, though, is too charitable, for
Teterevka is not only paralyzed by folly but is crippled by knavery;
and while Benjamin remains a fool, his charitable outlook, his feeling that what he is doing is for all Jews, makes him far superior to
the morally limited residents of Teterevka.

The other large city that Benjamin and Senderel visit is a town we
already know, Glupsk. As we should expect, Glupsk differs little
from the other towns, and the first sight we have of Glupsk is of two
old women discussing their visit to a fortuneteller. Their conversation is interrupted by a commotion in the street, which, we soon
learn, has been caused by the arrival of the Red Jews, actually
Benjamin and Senderel, who "had won the confidence of certain
pious Jews, just as a miracle-mongering cobbler had done only a
short time before" (88). These pious Jews are two old women whose
daily practice it was to wait at the city limits in case the Messiah
should come. As Mendele says, the "explorers had at last come upon
fellow Jews who really appreciated them. And it is only Glupsk that
could duly appreciate and esteem so fine a pair" (88–89). Benjamin
and Senderel have traveled from Tuneyadevka—Droneville—to
Glupsk—Foolstown; in short, they have not made much progress in
their journey, but have simply managed to survey the various kinds
of paralysis that afflicted the Jewish world. It is significant that this
journey has Glupsk as its last city, for Glupsk—Berdichev—was, as
we recall, the site of another example of paralysis, the "action" of *Di
Takse*. This reappearance of Glupsk undercuts to a degree those
critics who elevate the humor of *Benjamin the Third* over its satire,
for the whole journey has been leading up to this city, about which
Abramovitsh had such good reason to be bitter, both on his own
account and on account of the whole Jewish situation. His description of the town, seen through Benjamin's eyes, begins with humor,
but quickly develops into a bitter commentary. On approaching the
town, the traveler must first jump over a succession of mud holes
and then pass by a mound of rubbish, where a single cow grazes and
occasionally sighs, "as though deploring the bitter lot of those
passers-by and at the same time lamenting her own, for having
fallen into the hands of some Jew or other" (90). Benjamin then
describes, in a marvelous passage, the marketplace of Glupsk, with
its crowd of hucksters, customers, and thieves; and then, in a passage reminiscent of Abramovitsh's earlier works, he describes the
castes into which the town is divided. These include

the class of Grabbers, who rule the town with a firm hand; then there is the class of Paper Shufflers, who use any weapon to defend the Grabbers against their enemies and who earn, thereby, a secure living and free meat. Below these comes the class of Distorters, who will dupe anyone while steering a straight course themselves. These are subdivided into the Swaggerers, worldly men who interfere in business matters, and the Two-Faced, hypocrites who interfere in religious matters. The lowest division comprises the class of the Foolish and Fearful-Silent and Straitened, the common crowd, which submits to the other classes and receives in return an eternity of plague.[11]

This is the Glupsk we remember from the earlier works, the Glupsk that is basically divided into two classes: knaves and fools. The biggest difference in this description of the town is that it emphasizes how foolish even the knaves are, thus providing the appearance of humor, though we must never forget the knavery. Thus, on the basis of an ancient coin whose surfaces have been rubbed almost smooth, and using a great deal of fanciful speculation, the citizens of Glupsk trace their ancestry back to the Jews who were sent by King Solomon to Ophir, and who later settled on the shores of Lake Pyatignilovka—Lake Fivefold Foul. These qualities of knavery, foolishness, and false pride combine to produce again the paralysis that characterizes *Benjamin the Third.*

The worst example of paralysis, however, comes near the end of the book, where we see Benjamin and Senderel taken in by the *khappers,* the kidnappers who turn our poor heroes over to the army. It should be emphasized that there really were such people: because serving in the czar's army was such torture for the Jews (and the army was often used to separate the Jews from their religion), rich families would often pay a poor person to enlist as a means of protecting their own children, or, as in *Benjamin the Third,* pay people to kidnap substitute victims. Occasionally, as in Axenfeld's early drama *The First Jewish Recruit* or Abramovitsh's second play *The Draft,* the corrupt community leaders would protect their sons at the expense of innocent but poor families. All of this trickery was encouraged by the czarist government, which quite rightly recognized that such methods would breed disharmony among the Jews; and it is no accident that Benjamin and Senderel meet the *khappers* in Glupsk, for here we have the first example of real viciousness in the book. Up to this point, the paralysis that we have seen has

consisted largely of inaction, but now we have a clear example of
moral paralysis, as we see Jews having their fellow Jews kidnapped
to serve in place of their own children. In their attempt to save
themselves, they were actually destroying any chance of continuing
their existence as Jews. At this point, paralysis has turned into
suicide. So stultified are the people that they have begun to feed on
themselves, and the novel's humor becomes black indeed.

A final instance of paralysis concerns the state of religion. As we
saw earlier, Abramovitsh was a religious man, but he was also aware
that too great a reliance on the direct intervention of God could lead
to human inaction. He once said that "our whole misfortune is that
spirituality has undermined our footing; we are left without a foundation. We have to be more interested in material things, sink our
roots into the earth. . . ."[12] This does not mean that he would abandon the religion (which he did not) or that he would stop saying
those prayers that refer to the coming of the Messiah or the rebuild-
ing of Israel, but only that those beliefs and desires that religious
Jews share should be implemented by real human action here in the
world.

The question of religion also brings up the subject of the Talmud,
that complex and intricate work that formed—and forms—the
center of orthodox Jewish life. Abramovitsh, as a young man, was a
prodigy in the study of Talmud and had the greatest respect for it;
but he also realized that the exclusive study of the Talmud was
partially responsible for the wide gulf between the Jewish and non-
Jewish worlds—for the paralysis. A good example of this aspect of
the problem is Reb Aaron Yossele, the son of Sarah Zlata, the rabbi
of Tuneyadevka: " 'Why—no trifle, this! It was rumored that in his
youth he had actually studied fractions!' " (20–21). The whole sense
of the book—much motion with little progress—can be felt in Reb
Aaron Yossele's contribution to the discussion of Benjamin's alleged
madness:

Teh, teh, teh—and again *teh*! It's true that Benjamin isn't bright—very far
from it. But from that it doesn't follow that he's mad, either. For the moot
point arises: Why has he gone mad precisely now and not before? Furthermore, why not last summer, or the summer before that, when the heat was
much worse? What's the inference, you ask? The inference is . . . well,
take our lake, for instance. Our lake, as everybody knows, has claimed one
life, annually, from time immemorial, and yet in recent years it hasn't
claimed a single victim. On the contrary, the lake itself has dropped so low

during the past few years that there are places in it where you can cross it practically dry-shod. But what's that got to do with Benjamin, you ask? Oh, what people! (24–25)

The style here parodies Talmudic discourse, with its strict insistence on logic, on questioning, and on elaborating the problems; but Reb Aaron Yossele is incapable of using these methods to get anywhere, and in fact part of the humor lies in his having applied Talmudic methods to so comic and trivial a figure as Benjamin. He simply cannot approach the question in a straightforward way and deliver a straightforward answer because he is trapped in his Talmudism. Similarly, when he later accompanies Senderel's wife on her search for her husband, he allows the travelers to escape when he launches into a Talmudic discussion in the middle of a heavily traveled bridge. He is a learned, respected, well-intentioned man who can put none of his good qualities to any practical use, though it seems he is always trying. All the paralysis of the novel is distilled in his brief appearances.

This rather serious discussion of the novel's major theme has perhaps ignored some of the book's considerable humor, but the humor is there to underscore the problems. The people we meet are foolish, and foolishness often makes us laugh. But when we realize exactly what we are laughing at—when we think of the causes and the effects of the foolishness—the humor turns into black humor and our laughter at least changes character. As Abramovitsh said, again in response to the postcard from Bialik and Ravnitzki, " 'When Sholem Aleichem describes something sad, he himself laughs. And I—my heart pains me. When you tell a joke or make a smart remark, your listener laughs, not you. And I—I cry; I can't laugh!' "[13] We can laugh while we read *Benjamin the Third*, but we must examine our laughter.

III *Benjamin and Senderel*

Paulson says that among the important aspects of *Don Quixote* are "the intention of questioning outmoded patterns of thought, the technique of confronting romance with realism, and the ambiguous attitude toward the protagonist."[14] All are obvious in *Benjamin the Third*. The first we have already seen as one of the causes of paralysis, but the last two are especially apparent in regard to Benjamin himself. Part of Benjamin's ambiguity lies in his being simultaneously the idealist and the fool. He cannot simply be dismissed as a fool because he is a sincere idealist whose ideals have real merit; on the other hand, his ideals are undercut by his folly. Thus Benjamin's actions have the appearance of lunacy, but when Mendele quotes him, he sounds completely rational—or, at least, no more foolish than anyone else in the book. He is not a lunatic, not even as much of a lunatic as Don Quixote, though like the Don he has his *idée fixe*: his determination to be a world traveler and to find the Red Jews, to be like his hero, Alexander the Great. " 'Tuneyadevka and Macedonia—two glorious places, destined to enjoy an equal fame, because of Alexander of Tuneyadevka and Benjamin of Macedon—or is it the other way around? . . .' " (28).

Much of Benjamin's foolishness, however, can be attributed to innocence. Early in the narrative Mendele tells us that Benjamin was like "a chick in its shell, or a worm in horseradish. He had a notion that the world's end lay just beyond Tuneyadevka . . ." (20). Furthermore, we learn that "life in his home town seemed to Benjamin to be good and glorious, even though he lived in poverty and his wife and children went around in rags. However, had Adam and Eve been disconcerted by the fact of their being naked and barefooted while they were still in the Garden of Eden?" (21). Like a chick in its shell and like Adam and Eve in Eden, Benjamin is completely innocent and naive, but he is also pure and uncorrupted. He expects to win fame, but he is essentially unselfish. The other, and more important part of his folly lies in his believing all the fantastic books he reads and then thinking that all this reading has provided him with the experience he needs. In this he is not very different from Isrulik, whose philosophy was based on an idealism divorced from the realities of the world, though Isrulik finally learned to face those realities. Benjamin, however, is almost totally oblivious to any realities. He is the Maskil carried a step further, emphasizing romance over reality. Whereas Isrulik believed that all problems could be solved by following Haskala theory, Benjamin fails to recognize most problems, seeing all obstacles as part of the great romance he is living. As we have seen, he compares himself to Joseph in Egypt and to Alexander the Great; and when, early in their journey, Senderel says that he will follow Benjamin " 'as a calf follows its dam,' " Benjamin sees himelf "as a captain steering his ship through turbulent seas. Just the same, the praise had not blinded him to the stark reality of his having no idea of where they were and the possibility that they might have gone astray" (55). Such a trifling problem, however, cannot stop a hero who has set out with no provisions and no idea of how to reach his goal.

Benjamin's ambiguity is also emphasized by Mendele, who twice compares him to Columbus, as in the following:

There are millions now living happily in America, yet Columbus, its discoverer, had plenty of grief in his time and was held up to scorn by his contemporaries. Our Benjamin of Tuneyadevka fared no better. His very appearance stamped him as an eccentric, and his talk of his projected journey elicited only mirth and derision. Fortunately for the world Benjamin didn't quite perceive the coolness of his reception; otherwise he might, God forbid, have become exasperated to the point of illness and abandoned his grandiose plans. And just think what the world would have lost then! (78–79)

Obviously the comparison between the two travelers is ludicrous, and yet Columbus was, in fact, regarded as a madman by his contemporaries. Furthermore, Columbus' discovery of America resulted in the creation of the United States, where many Jews fled during Abramovitsh's time in order to escape from the persecutions of Europe and the Pale. Thus on the one hand we have paralysis and foolishness, and on the other we have sincerity, good intentions, and some kind of attempt, however wrongheaded, to end the Jews' sufferings.

One of the reasons that *Benjamin the Third* is so often considered to be primarily a humorous book lies in Abramovitsh's efforts to illustrate Benjamin's folly. There are so many examples that it is difficult to choose among them. At one point, for instance, Benjamin dreams that he is bending over to whisper an important secret to the rabbi and he awakens to find himself hugging a calf ("How had a calf come to be here? Could it be that he, Benjamin, had calved?" [59]), who subsequently overturns a tub of water on our hero's head. Another example, which appears several times, is Benjamin's ignorance of the Russian language. When he is lost in the woods, when he is on the road with Senderel, and when the two of them venture out on Lake Pyatignilovka, he cannot deal with the Russians he meets. And although Senderel supposedly knows the language, he is hardly fluent. Nevertheless, when one of the peasants they meet does not understand Senderel's unintelligible questions, Benjamin instructs his companion to " 'tell him more distinctly—he's got only

a peasant's head on his shoulders' " (56). Here again there is ambiguity: the scene is funny and Benjamin is a fool; and yet Benjamin,
who cannot speak the peasant's language, the language of the country in which he himself lives, regards him condescendingly. There is
humor in this episode, but there is also the tragedy of paralysis, for
the great world traveler cannot even communicate with his fellow
countrymen.

The folly (and tragedy) of our heroes is also illustrated in their
relationships with their wives. Both of them are henpecked and
both of their wives appear to be horrifying shrews, stereotypes of
the nagging, domineering female. This appearance, however, requires examination. Northrop Frye says that a central theme of
satire is "the disappearance of the heroic. This is the main reason for
the predominance in fictional satire of what may be called the Om-
phale archetype, the man bullied or dominated by women. . . ."[15]
We saw in *Ha'avot Vehabanim* and *Dos Kleyne Mentshele* how Abramovitsh treated the unfortunate role of women in the *shtetl*, and
the wives in *Benjamin the Third* are products of the same de-
humanizing conditions. Both wives support their families, while the
husbands do whatever they choose, including running away to find
the Red Jews. Benjamin "spent all his time in the synagogue, and it
was his wife who provided for the household, running a small shop
that she had set up. . . . Not that her entire stock in trade
amounted to much; if, in addition to the shop, she hadn't also managed to knit stockings, pluck feathers during the evening, and ac-
cumulate rendered chicken fat for resale on the eve of Passover
. . . they wouldn't have been able to keep body and soul together"
(35). Nevertheless, though she takes care of all the practical matters
while her husband reads romances and fancies himself a Jewish
Alexander the Great, she is regarded with scorn ("A housewife, be
she even as full of virtues as a biblical matron, still remained nothing
more than a simple housewife." [36]), and when Benjamin leaves on
his journey, he thinks to himself, " 'My wife—praised be His
Name!—I have provided for . . ." (47). The household of Senderel
the Housewife, as he is known, is in a similar condition. Even on
this level we can understand why the wives would be shrews, but
the horror of their situation goes even deeper. Because of the traditional relationship between the sexes, both women are dependent
on their husbands. When Benjamin is lost in the woods, Zelda
becomes hysterical; and Senderel's wife even journeys with the

rabbi to bring Senderel back to Tuneyadevka. Both women are afraid of being *agunot*, women whose husbands either abandoned them or died without witnesses, for the position of the *agunah* was one of shame and helplessness.[16] Is it any wonder, then, that Mendele can speak of the housewives' "customary round of bickering with their husbands, spanking the children, and hanging out the bedclothes to air" (48)? The two wives are among the strongest, most practical characters in the book, yet they are kept in a subservient and degraded position by their foolish husbands, they are paralyzed by the traditional view of women as inferior beings. Again, something that is superficially humorous turns out to be truly tragic.

Through most of the book, then, Benjamin may be right when he describes Senderel and himself as " 'body and soul. While you concern yourself with corporeal matters, such as provender for our journey, I look after things spiritual' " (54), but together they form the equivalent of a fool—created, no doubt, by their environment, but still a fool. They are clearly, as Ruth Wisse demonstrates, in the tradition of the *schlemiel*.

IV   *The Conclusion*

Thus far we have seen *Benjamin the Third* concentrate on the problem within the Jewish community—not the active evil of *Dos Kleyne Mentshele* or *Di Takse*, but the paralysis, the stagnation, the lack of a sense of direction, of contact with the real world that beset Russian Jewry. All this has been done humorously, but with satiric and even tragic undertones. At the novel's end, however, a strange transformation occurs. Isrulik spent most of his time in *Di Klyatshe* criticizing the Jews and only gradually learned to look at the outside world as the source of the problems; and in *Benjamin the Third*, Mendele takes us, his readers, on a similar journey, for once Benjamin and Senderel are forced into the Russian army, once we see how the authorities treat them, their paralysis and folly appear in another light. Ruth Wisse describes this transformation very well: "For the better part of the book, he [Benjamin] embodies all the psychological and historical weaknesses the author is ridiculing, and Mendele spares no comic or satiric devices in holding these weaknesses up to view. Then, almost without warning, Benjamin in his simplicity becomes a serious moral alternative to the organized evil that would destroy him."[17] Just as the nag revealed the truth to

Isrulik, so Mendele reveals it to us. Isrulik's description of the Jews is correct, as is Mendele's: they are paralyzed and foolish. And yet the story is not complete without a consideration of the outside pressures—official government anti-Semitism, for example—that have led to this paralysis. Certainly Benjamin cannot speak Russian; but it was the government's policy to exclude Jews from the mainstream of Russian life. This is why the Pale of Settlement existed at all. Again, seen in this light, the humor of the book—and it is abundant—suddenly becomes overtly tragic.

This change is apparent in the new relationship between Benjamin and Senderel when they are in the army. Both, of course, are incompetent soldiers; but Senderel really tries to succeed, while Benjamin expresses his disgust, and it is Benjamin, the idealist, who proposes that they try to escape. When they are caught and thrown in jail to await a court martial, Senderal literally becomes a dreamer, dreaming that his grandfather brings him toys, while Benjamin, suddenly a serious figure, worries about completing his journey. Just as Senderel was content in Tuneyadevka and content on the road with Benjamin, so he is now content to accept imprisonment; but Benjamin, the idealist whose ambition it was to escape from the confines of Tuneyadevka, suffers even more anguish in prison. "In his agony he fidgeted about, clutched at his head and murmured: 'What harm did I ever do them! Good God, what do they want of me?' " (121). It is no accident that he sounds here like the nag, and we realize that this is the question we must ask throughout the book. The problems of *Benjamin the Third* are the problems of *Di Klyatshe* seen from another point of view, lulling us into thinking like Isrulik and suddenly making us aware that our answers are too simple, too pat. The Tuneyadevka chief of police did not act alone in persecuting the Jews. Rather he was part of a whole bureaucracy whose job it was to see that the Tuneyadevkars remained Tuneyadevkars; and however foolish and misguided Benjamin's plans are, they are also, in a way, noble. Abramovitsh recognizes the cause of paralysis, but urges the people to take action. That he offers no specific program is not odd, for satire's job is to criticize, not necessarily to offer solutions. He knows that he must at least rouse the people by making them aware of their situation, and this task he accomplishes.

There is here, then, as in all Quixotic fiction, a tension between the supposed insanity of the Quixote figure and the supposed sanity of the other characters, in this case both the Jewish and non-Jewish ones. Abramovitsh builds this tension throughout the novel, bringing it to a head in the army scenes. Because this tension is unresolvable, and because he has transformed Benjamin so drastically from fool to hero, he can only end the book, which he does by having the travelers discharged from the army on the grounds of incompetence. Benjamin both is and is not a fool; the Jewish world both is and is not practical and level-headed. Both, to a certain extent, can only be defined in relation to the hostile outside world, which leaves us with Benjamin's questions: " 'What harm did I ever do them! Good God, what do they want of me?' " Beneath the poverty, the foolishness, the superstition, and the paralysis lies nobility, just as the external form of the nag conceals a king's son. At the end of *Benjamin the Third* we get a glimpse of that nobility. As Faulkner says of Dilsey in *The Sound and the Fury*, "They endured." The Benjamins and Senderels and Zeldas and rabbis and Heikel the Stammerers endured, in spite of their folly, their paralysis, and, most important of all, in spite of their oppressors.

CHAPTER 6

Fishke der Krumer:
A Time to Embrace

I   Der Priziv

THE period following the publication of *Benjamin the Third* in 1878 was one of the darkest in Abramovitsh's life. In 1879 he issued the revised version of *Dos Kleyne Mentshele*, but family problems and political events put such a strain on him that he produced no new work worth mentioning until 1884. The family problems, of course, were distressing, for his daughter died suddenly and his son was arrested for taking part in political protests. One bright spot was that Abramovitsh's chronic poverty was relieved when, in 1881, he was made the principal of a modern Jewish school in Odessa. This job was naturally most welcome, but it took a great deal of Abramovitsh's energy, as he directed the teaching, raised funds, and worked generally at making the school a success, putting his ideas about education into practice, leaving little time for writing. As he wrote to Sholem Aleichem in 1903, "You tell me to take a lesson from Tolstoy. That's a joke. Let your Tolstoy try to be a Jew for a few days, let alone a teacher in a Talmud Torah. . . . Oy, when you've got a Yasnaya Polyana and all those other good things, then you can shove everything aside and write, write, write!"[1]

The political events, however, had an even more important influence on his work, for they reflected the situation he had already described and they shaped the course that his later work would follow. In short, what happened was the assassination of Czar Alexander II, in March 1881. After the anti-Semitic excesses of Nicholas I, Alexander seemed to be the most benevolent of monarchs. In the course of his reign, the Jews made rapid advances in numerous fields, since they were now allowed to attend Russian schools and take up some previously restricted occupations. The lot of the common people was still most difficult, but at least the future

108

seemed a little brighter. This period of hopefulness, however, proved to be only a brief respite, for even while Alexander was alive, the anti-Jewish press began calling attention to Jewish advances, marshaling public opinion against the Jews. Thus, when Alexander was assassinated and one of the revolutionaries who was arrested turned out to be Jewish, all the Jews' progress proved to be illusory. The new czar, Alexander III, and his chief adviser, Constantin Pobiedonostsev, inaugurated their reign with government-sponsored pogroms, which resulted in horrible massacres of Jews throughout Russia. The dream of a better life in Russia turned into a tragic nightmare, and thousands upon thousands of the survivors simply gave up and left for America, a course that required great courage and determination. The Jews who, like Abramovitsh, remained in Russia, were almost totally dispirited. The promises of the Haskala were shattered. All the things that the people had been led to expect were again out of reach, all the more tantalizing because they had once seemed so close. It was as though the Jews were being told that if they ever tried to rise above their station again, they would again be beaten down. All their hopes for a better life disappeared and they were left with nothing but despair.

In such circumstances, it is hardly surprising that Abramovitsh could not bring himself to write. How could he even pretend to write Haskalic literature; how could he urge his people to better their lot? It was as though Benjamin had discovered what a fool he was and had reformed, studying seriously, taking care of his family, learning Russian, trying to raise himself above his inherited station, only to be attacked more viciously and violently by the Tuneyadevka police chief, beaten over the head until he again assumed the character of a fool. As Abramovitsh wrote to his friend Binshtok in March of 1881: "I completely agree with Rousseau, who urged man to throw his stupid civilization to the devil and turn back to the forests."[2]

For three years after the massacres, Abramovitsh largely abandoned his writing, unable to continue, until in 1884 he published his second and last play, *Der Priziv (The Draft)*. In the preface to the play he discusses his long silence and describes his new way of looking at the world: "Jewish children have no anxiety about troubles, thank God. They've had every kind of trouble for the last few thousand years, just like they have now. When these troubles will end, only God knows. Meanwhile, one can only be a human being.

One looks around, laughs, plays, and even does a little jig."[3] (Significantly, in the late 1880s, he worked hard at trying again to better Russian-Jewish relations.) There is not much laughter and dancing in *Der Priziv*, and on the whole it is not a very good play, but at least it broke Abramovitsh's silence. This play, reminiscent of Axenfeld's *Der Ershter Yidisher Rekrut*, has many of the same problems as *Di Takse* without the passionate feeling that gave some life to the earlier play. A much more resigned work, *Der Priziv* tells the story of Reizeleh, the daughter of a rich family, and Alexander, her fiance. Through various machinations, he is drafted into the army and is eventually reported to be dead, at which point Reizeleh sacrifices herself by marrying a wealthy but repulsive man in order to save her father from financial ruin. As the play ends, Alexander returns and explains that the report of his death was obviously wrong, but it is too late for the lovers, who are to be kept apart forever. Throughout we see the schemes of various town leaders, including Reizeleh's father, much as we have seen them in earlier works; but we also see the courtship of two servants, Mendel (not to be confused with Mendele) and Dvossia, whose marriage appears to be happy and fairly prosperous, and who are among the most compassionate characters in the play. Like so many of Abramovitsh's works in which Mendele plays no part, *Der Priziv* must be accounted a failure,[4] its entire significance lying in its being Abramovitsh's first work in so many years.

Another work published in 1884 was Abramovitsh's translation and adaptation of Leon Pinsker's brief work "Autoemancipation," entitled in the Yiddish "A Remedy for Jewish Troubles." Although Abramovitsh was neither a Zionist nor a Territorialist, he certainly supported Pinsker's move for Jewish solidarity. His translation, however, differs considerably from Pinsker's text, for Abramovitsh transformed Pinsker's Germanic tone into everyday Yiddish in his attempt (despite his satiric attacks on the Haskala) to bring enlightenment to the masses. In addition, Pinsker's Territorialist goals are somewhat muted in the translation, with more emphasis being given to Jewish brotherhood and to exhortations to be strong: "Let us be men, Jewish children! Let us be men of determination and of strong character."[5] Abramovitsh's willingness to translate and inject his own ideas into this article indicate that his Rousseauesque despair with civilization was only temporary. Once again he was working for the betterment of the Jewish people in Russia, knowing full well that it was not practical for several million impoverished Jews to move to a land of their own.

Another work that Abramovitsh published in 1886–1887 was a Hebrew short story, "Beseter Ra'am" ("In the Secret Place of Thunder"). It is interesting that after twenty years he returned to Hebrew as his language of composition. It almost seems that, after the disaster of 1881, he realized that his primary function was no longer just the education of the masses but also the education of the disheartened Maskilim. This story consists of two slightly related chapters. The first is a long, half-comical, half-serious survey of Glupsk. It contains much of the old criticism, but in a far less strident way. The second chapter describes the results of the pogroms in Kabtzansk (Pauperville), where Mendele is stranded when his horse and wagon are stolen. Here Mendele describes the effects not only on the Jews but also on the non-Jews, who depend on the Jews for their livelihood. He also shows, in what was to become a dominant theme in his later works (though it was present throughout his writings), the dissension that split and weakened the Jewish community, the complete chaos caused by the pogroms. Mendele finally gets a new horse and wagon and leaves Kabtzansk, but he has been much more personally involved, is much closer to the people, than he has been heretofore.

II   Fishke der Krumer—*Introduction*

This motif was picked up in Abramovitsh's next novel, *Fishke der Krumer (Fishke the Lame)*, which is, quite simply, a masterpiece. Along with *Di Klyatshe* and *Benjamin the Third* it is one of the works that critics hail as being among Abramovitsh's greatest achievements. Actually, just as *Benjamin* marks a departure from *Di Klyatshe*, so *Fishke* marks a new period in Abramovitsh's creative life. In fact, with *Fishke* we move into his fourth major literary period. The first period produced Abramovitsh's early Hebrew, experimental works. The second marked his entrance into the field of social criticism and includes the writing of *Dos Kleyne Mentshele, Di Takse,* and *Di Klyatshe,* those bitterly satirical, didactic works. The third period, represented by *Benjamin the Third,* was the briefest, but was also in a sense the most positive, for in *Benjamin the Third* much of his Juvenalian railing had been transformed into a Horatian smile. In *Benjamin* the problems, especially those within the Jewish community, seem more manageable, seem almost capable of solution. We can more clearly see the king's son inside the nag. The book reflects, in essence, the political advances made under Alexander II: conditions are still bad, there are still clearly discernible evils, but it is also possible to see humor, to feel a little bit hopeful, to see the Jews in a more positive light. But then came 1881 and the pogroms—laughter stopped and hope disappeared; the Jewish people, having achieved new heights, sank lower than ever. Bitter social criticism would have been too cruel, and Horatian laughter would have been out of place, so Abramovitsh sought another mode. The result was *Fishke der Krumer,* in which, as Viner says, Abramovitsh both "celebrated the people as no one before him had and berated them for their backwardness. He was truthful rather than romantic."[6]

Actually, as with so many of Abramovitsh's works, there are several versions of *Fishke.* The first version dates from 1869, the year of *Di Takse,* and is little more than a long short story. The second version was written in the 1870s but was never published. The third Yiddish version was published in 1888 and forms the basis of the present study.[7] A final version appeared in 1907, and as usual, Abramovitsh later issued a Hebrew translation of the work, which he called *Sefer Hakabtzanim (The Beggar Book).* In terms of pure literary artistry, in terms of the control that Abramovitsh had over his materials, *Fishke* is unquestionably his greatest work. It is a beautiful, moving novel that can stand comparison with some of the great works in world literature; and its greatness is all the more remarkable in light of Abramovitsh's position as the pioneer of Yiddish literature. Clearly he was influenced by writers such as Swift, Sterne, Fielding, Dickens, Sue, Hugo, Dumas, Gogol, and others, but the genius that enabled him to use these writers in order to fashion a distinctively Jewish-Yiddish literature cannot be praised too highly.

The action of *Fishke* can be divided into two almost equal parts, the frame story and the story of Fishke. The story begins early in the morning of the seventeenth of Tammuz, the fast day that commemorates the beginning of the sieges of Jerusalem by Nebuchadnezzar and Titus and that comes exactly three weeks before the most mournful of all Jewish fast days, the Ninth of Ab, the day that commemorates the destruction of the First and Second Temples. Mendele, our narrator, tells us that he was traveling toward Glupsk, anticipating an increase in his business due to the arrival of the

period of mourning when Jews need "Books of Lamentations, Penitential Prayer Books, women's Books of Supplications, ram's horns
for the Day of Atonement, and prayer books for festivals" (17).
While he was traveling, he was busy saying his morning prayers, but
he was constantly being tempted to admire the natural beauty
around him, a temptation to which he quickly succumbed. A short
time later, having dozed off, he awoke to find his carriage stuck in
the mud, entangled with another carriage whose driver had also
apparently fallen asleep. The two drivers began to argue and fight,
until they recognized each other, the second driver being Alter
Yaknehoz, another bookseller. Naturally the fight stopped, and the
two decided to travel on together. As they were trying to free their
carts from the mud, they were both mocked and helped by some
passing peasants. Soon the two friends pulled off the road to rest and
talk, and Alter began telling his troubles. Like most Jews, Alter was
quite poor and would do anything he could, within reason, to get
money, for his oldest daughter needed a dowry and his young
wife—he had divorced his first wife—was expecting another child.
One of his moneymaking schemes, he explained, had just backfired:
while he was at one of the local fairs, he saw two old acquaintances of
his and he determined to serve as a matchmaker, to arrange a wedding between their children. Only after he had gone to a great deal
of trouble and gotten both fathers interested did he find out that
each father had only sons to marry off. Consequently he was in a bad
mood. Mendele, in an attempt to cheer up his friend, told him
about another funny match, that between the lame bathhouse attendant Fishke and a blind beggar girl.

Although Fishke was a well-known cripple in Glupsk, he was so
self-effacing that even when cripples were selected as "cholera
grooms."[8] he was always passed over. One day, however, when the
prospective groom of a blind woman refused to go through with the
ceremony, Fishke was recruited and suddenly found himself with a
wife. Although Mendele found the story humorous, Alter could
think only of his business, so that, in a very famous scene, the two
merchants traded merchandise, each convinced that he had come
out ahead, though no money had changed hands.

After the trade, Alter went to find their horses, who had wandered away; but when he failed to return Mendele, who had broken
his fast by drinking too much brandy, went to find him, in spite of
his slightly drunken fear of being alone in the woods. Eventually,

after a run-in with a Russian official who cut off one of his side curls, Mendele arrived at an inn, whose landlady, Chaya-Traina, turned out to be a distant relative of his. The next day Mendele fought off the landlady's attempts to make a match between her daughter and his son, and he arrived back at the wagons to find Alter, the horses, and, of all people, Fishke, whom Alter had found tied up in an old building, near which he also found their horses. Mendele, of course, was curious to hear Fishke's story, which, as retold by Mendele, takes up the rest of the novel.

After Fishke's marriage to the blind beggar, they were happy for a time; but soon she convinced him that they should leave Glupsk. They wandered unhappily around the country until they met a group of traveling beggars whose leader, red-headed Feibush, took a liking to Fishke's wife and made Fishke a miserable outcast. Fishke's only consolation was his friendship with Bayleh, a hunchback girl who traveled with the beggars after having been abandoned by her parents. Like Fishke, she was an outcast among the beggars. The rest of the novel shows the various tricks and evil deeds of the beggars and the growing love between Fishke and Bayleh, punctuated by a long digression in which Fishke, having been left behind by the group, describes his stay in Odessa. Finally, on his way back to Glupsk, Fishke encountered the beggars again, and he and Bayleh decided to run off together; but they were interrupted by Feibush, who tied Fishke up and left him to die. Fishke ended his story by bemoaning the fate of poor Bayleh; but Alter, who had been strangely quiet, announced that she was his daughter from his first marriage and that he would not rest again until he had rescued her. With that, he drove off, and Mendele and Fishke continued on to Glupsk.

Fishke der Krumer, presenting as it does an unbelievably complex picture of Jewish life, is Abramovitsh's most artistic novel. In the twenty-six years since his first attempt at fiction, both Abramovitsh and Yiddish literature had grown. Abramovitsh was finally capable of moving beyond the avowedly didactic aims of his earlier works. Not only had he made the social problems clear in those works, but he had done so in an increasingly artistic way, so that their didacticism (and didacticism is not necessarily a bad thing) had become more and more subtle. Also, as has become clear, he came increasingly to realize that education was not the solution to the Jewish situation, because the problems did not lie completely within the

Jewish people but were, rather, imposed upon them. In addition, thanks to his example, Yiddish literature no longer had to be didactic, no longer had to justify its existence on the grounds that it was there primarily to teach. Attention could be devoted to artistic matters.[9] That is why *Fishke* is more aesthetically pleasing than any of his other novels. His use of the frame story, for instance, is much more sophisticated than it had been in *Dos Kleyne Mentshele*, so that the seemingly irrelevant conversation between Mendele and Alter and the episode at the inn with Chaya-Traina are finally seen as integral parts of the narrative. There is no picaresque wandering in *Fishke* and there are no loose ends. Everything fits.

III *Mendele Mocher Seforim*

One of the most interesting aspects of *Fishke* is Mendele himself. In the earlier novels, Mendele had served merely as the printer or editor of someone else's work, even in the complex narrative of *Benjamin the Third*. We got to know something about him from his various introductions and occasional interjections, but what we got to know was colored by his well-thought-out cynicism. He distanced himself from the Jewish community, yet he printed the works because of his great love for the people, because of his sense of outrage at their plight. As in *Benjamin the Third*, his cynicism always evolved into a kind of identification with its object, so that Benjamin, finally, is not only to be laughed at as a fool, for Mendele has maneuvered us into such a position that both we and he identify with the poor hero. Mendele, however, only became a central character in "Beseter Ra'am"; and we see even more of him in *Fishke*, where we got to know him better than ever.

At the novel's beginning, Mendele is in his favorite position, driving his wagon alone through the countryside, admiring, in spite of himself, the natural beauties around him. Almost everyone who writes about Abramovitsh, especially among older critics, comments on his descriptions of nature, for natural beauty was not an important part of Jewish life. In Eastern Europe the Jews' separation from nature was reinforced by the dirty, suffocating *shtetl* and the Jews' understandable reluctance to walk through the woods or even to wander along the roads. But Abramovitsh loved nature and natural beauty, and his first work, it should be remembered, was the translation of a book on natural history. He endowed Mendele with this same love, though Mendele is torn between his human feelings and

the traditional view that natural beauty was something to be ignored. Of course his human feelings win out, but what we see is the
debate between his Good Impulse and his Evil Impulse, interspersed with lengthy descriptions of the natural beauty that has
tempted him. In all the works in which he had appeared, he expressed cynical—or at least ambiguous—opinions about God's role
in the world, about his beliefs as a Jew. Here he is engaged in the
same game, though he becomes most upset when his internal battle
results in his making a mistake in his prayers. His cynicism seems to
be a cover, something he uses to conceal his true thoughts, though
his mistake resulted not simply from admiring nature but from his
feelings of guilt at wanting to admire it. Thus, that same evening,
when Mendele and Alter are preparing to say the evening prayers,
he provides a long description of the breeze, the trees, the wheat in
the fields, the butterflies, the various songs of birds, frogs, bees,
flies, and crickets. " 'What a pleasure,' " he thinks, " 'to hear, see
and smell the sights, the odors all around' "; and he says to Alter,
" 'Reb Alter, it's beautiful! It makes your heart leap with joy. God's
world is alive! God's world is wonderful.' " Alter's response is the
response of the *shtetl*: " 'Reb Mendele, shame on you.' " Nevertheless, Mendele offers a beautiful description of the two of them pray-
ing at the roadside: "Thus we both sang our praises to His dear
Name, while all the bushes and flowers in the fields and all the birds
and beasts in the woods burst into song and gave their thanks to
God" (62). There is nothing cynical in this pastoral description, as
man and nature join to praise God. It is, in fact, one of the most
peaceful moments in Abramovitsh's works.

This does not mean, however, that Mendele has stopped questioning God's ways, as can be seen in the encounter between the
two Jews and the peasants who help them push their wagons out of
the mud. Mendele is quite fair in pointing out that without the
peasants, they could not have moved the wagons, and he is grateful
for their help, even to the point of belittling himself: the peasants
"pushed in real earnest, for the hands were the hands of Esau; but
with us it was only the voice, and the voice was the voice of Jacob.
We grunted and groaned and struggled as if we were really pushing. . . . But that's not my point" (24). Here we have the "beside
the point" game again, and it is clear that this is precisely his point.
He and Alter, both adept at using words, are incapable of moving

the wagons, and though they make a show of trying to be like the peasants, it is only a show. They simply cannot be like them. Thus, as the peasants leave, in spite of their kindness in helping, they turn around and yell, " 'Jewish swine.' " Alter ignores the insult, but Mendele is moved to address God:

"Almighty God . . . open Your eyes and look down from Heaven, and see how Your Godfearing Jews are subject to derision and shame for the sake of Your beloved Name, because they stand in awe of You, they respect Your commandments, proudly and sincerely. So pour down on us Your mercy and let us find favor and grace in Your eyes and in the eyes of all people. Shield Your beloved sheep. . . . Improve my luck for having praised and glorified Your Name today in reverence. And send to me, Your servant Mendele . . . and to all Israel, a small livelihood, a good little business with joy in our souls, Amen!"[10]

Mendele is truly offended by the anti-Semitic insult, and he wonders sincerely at the trials that the Jews must undergo simply for being Jewish; but *Di Klyatshe* taught that one must eat before he can do tricks, and so Mendele concludes his prayer in what seems at first a sacrilegious way, by asking that business should be good. But this is neither sacrilege nor greed. It is quite simply a plea that he may earn his livelihood that day. "It is true," he seems to say, "that it is hard to be a Jew; but we are Jews and, for some reason we cannot understand, we suffer for it. Let us at least hold body and soul together." This is not the old cynical side of Mendele that we have seen so often. It is Mendele asking, in a modified way, the question of Job, the questions of the nag and of Benjamin—why do we suffer?—and then, in the absence of a comprehensible answer, moving on to a matter of practical concern, his ability to earn a living. But as we shall see, Jewish life was indeed capable of rising above this necessary level. Mendele hints at the possibilities in his descriptions of nature, but Fishke's story will offer dramatic and poignant proof.

Mendele is also at his most introspective in *Fishke*. Externally he still maintains a certain distance between himself and the Jewish masses, but in his private thoughts the distinctions melt away and we can see him within the Jewish community. This process begins rather unobtrusively when he tells us why he likes the heat of this very hot day so much:

Because I love to perspire, I would have enjoyed the heat if the sun were not beating directly into my eyes: I could lie for hours on the upper bench in the steam bath in the very greatest heat. My father, his memory be praised, had accustomed me to it even as a child. He was a hot, smoldering, burning, fiery Jew. He loved to steam himself through and through and thereby made a name for himself. He was greatly beloved among the people, for the very gist of Jewishness is to be found in this fiery nature. Therefore they regarded him as a respectable Jew who was close to God. They spoke of him with reverence:

"Oh, yes, as far as whipping goes, he is a deep scholar. He's a past master on the subject 'steam bath.' He knows . . . he knows all there is to know about sweating!"

Sweating is a Jewish thing. Not a Sabbath goes by, not a holiday, when a Jew does not find himself in a good sweat. Who, among all the seventy nations of the world, has sweated more than the Jews? But that's not my point. (28–29)

Again, what is his point if not the history of Jewish "sweating" in which he includes himself? He may not have his father's fiery nature, but he can, metaphorically, "take the heat." His meditation about his own past here moves subtly to a consideration of the Jewish situation, the further exploration of which is one of the novel's major themes; and it is no accident that Fishke, before his marriage, was a bathhouse attendant. This is not the bathhouse of *Benjamin the Third*, a gathering place for do-nothings. It is, rather a metaphor for Jewish existence, a place where one sweats as the Jews have sweated throughout their history; and Fishke, the crippled bathhouse attendant, who occupies the lowest rung among this lowest of nations, has spent more time than anyone else in the bathhouse. Thus Mendele's nostalgia at this point reverberates throughout the novel and out into real Jewish life.

Similarly, when the Russian official cuts off one of Mendele's sidecurls, all of his cynicism disappears:

Seeing my prayer curl on the floor, I burst into tears—my old, gray prayer curl which has been with me from childhood until now; my prayer curl which had shared the joys and pains of an entire lifetime! Why, my mother had fondled it, combed it, and took pride in its shiny black waves when I was a boy. It was an adornment on my face in days gone by, when I was young and fresh. The poor thing became prematurely gray from troubles and worry, and I was not, God forfend, one bit ashamed of its grayness. We had both aged early from poverty, loneliness, afflictions, threats, uncalled-for enmity and persecution from the rest of the world. Oh whom, good Lord, had it offended? Whom, I ask, had my gray hairs harmed? (71)

So insulted is he by this outrage that he actually stands there and cries, until even the official comforts him: "It seems that a human heart beat under those brass buttons." This episode casts some light on the changes that Abramovitsh had undergone since the time of *Benjamin the Third*, for in that novel, one of the police chief's favorite tricks was to cut off sidecurls, and Mendele took some satiric enjoyment in describing the people's responses, their flight to the house of study or to the bathhouse where they could discuss things of absolutely no relevance to their situation. There Mendele laughed at them and pointed out the futility of their passivity. Mendele wanted some action on their part, a proper response, not a flight to refuge or a search for the Red Jews. Now, finding himself in the same situation, he thinks only of his poor sidecurl, of all it has been through with him, and he weeps.

This is not to say that weeping is an improper response. Mendele is not being hypocritical here. Rather, he has learned something about persecution and "uncalled-for enmity." The events of 1881, the blind hatred and brutality of the outside world, have taken their toll of Mendele's cynicism. What other response is there for one in his predicament? Again we are back to Job and the question of how we must respond to the inexplicable; and suddenly weeping does not appear to be such a bad response. As Mendele leaves the room, he uncynically picks up the curl and puts it in his pocket. He is not, at this point, the observer, standing back and observing the Jewish community. He is directly involved—his predicament is that of the whole community—and he behaves just as any of them might.

Perhaps Mendele's most introspective moment comes later that night at Chaya-Traina's inn. After all the events of the day, he cannot sleep because of the bedbugs, so he goes to the window for a moment. Here he sees the full moon, which "stirred up a sea of emotions within me. My thoughts were inclined to dwell on myself—thoughts about my bitter life with its fill of illness, humiliations, insults and injuries, both old and new" (84–85). This is not the Mendele of *Dos Kleyne Mentshele*, who hoped to find Gutman, or of *Benjamin the Third*, who laughed at his fellow Jews. This is a man who has seen the ugly side of human nature, who has seen pogroms, who has been humiliated through no fault of his own. Finally, he tells us, "I whimpered like a weak child before its mother: '*Oy*, Mama! My heart is black and blue. Haven't I had my share of headaches and bellyaches? . . . Haven't I had wounds enough already? Then why do they begrudge me a little peace and quiet?' " (85). Never have we seen Mendele so pathetic—never have we imagined that he could be so pathetic—but recent events have left their mark on him, and weeping again, he tells us, "I lay my head down on my arm, the side with the shorn side curl facing the moon: 'Here, look! See what they've done to me!' A well of pent-up feelings opened within me, roared into my heart and flooded my mind. I stared blankly into the void with my swollen eyes and begged: 'G'vald! Help me! Have mercy!' " (85).

Mendele, however, soon recovers from his abysmal despair, not by reasserting his old cynicism, but by recognizing a completely opposite feeling, "a wordless feeling of hope and cheer. Just such a feeling enters a Jew's soul after he has laid his troubles before God and has cried his eyes out over them! It is a feeling which makes a man . . . ready to embrace the entire world and kiss it—so overwhelming are his feelings of love" (85). He even develops compassion for the bedbugs. Somewhat like Job, he has received no explanation for the evils that have befallen him, but he is sustained by his faith. The relationship between Mendele—between any Jew—and God is a very close one. Here God is clearly the parent who, simply by hearing the child's plaint, provides comfort, even if He does not remove the actual pain. Still, this answer is a bit too pat, and while Mendele may feel comforted, his feelings will, as we shall see, be severely tested by Fishke.

In spite of this remarkable episode, Mendele still retains his cynical pose when he deals with other characters. Thus, when he describes the portraits hanging on Chaya-Traina's walls, he says that "Napoleon was there, too. He had also fallen into Jewish hands, poor man, Lord have mercy on his sad condition" (79). This is the same Mendele who in *Benjamin the Third* described a cow who occasionally sighed, lamenting the fate that allowed her to fall "into the hands of some Jew or other."[11] However close he feels to God in his moment of introspection, he knows that the Jewish condition is not enviable, and that their cows and even their pictures suffer. Similarly, Mendele is often quite cruel to Fishke as the poor cripple attempts to tell his story. He constantly makes fun of Fishke's speech impediment (impossible to duplicate in English), and he emphasizes that we are hearing the story in his words, since Fishke's are so nearly incomprehensible. Then he makes sarcastic comments about Fishke's story. When, for example, Fishke tells how he fell in love with Bayleh, Mendele is first struck by melancholy, and then, " 'Do you hear, Reb Alter?' I said with a little smile. 'Our Fishke is really head over heels in love with the hunchbacked girl. It's strange . . .' " (135). Mendele, who will later feel Fishke's story very deeply, is at this point as bad as the Russian official, as he denies Fishke's basic humanness. His attitude that it is funny for someone like Fishke to be in love corresponds exactly to the feelings of anti-Semites, who feel that the Jews, in their eyes the lowest of human beings, are incapable of feeling emotion—or even physical pain.[12] After Mendele's soul searching of the previous evening, his attitude toward Fishke, whom he basically likes, is most unbecoming; and when later he understands the full tragedy of Fishke's story, his attitude will change. But, as with his attitude toward women in *Dos Kleyne Mentshele*, he is at first oblivious to his own prejudices, and he only comes to understand them when they are pointed out rather forcefully. In both books he clearly goes through a learning process, and it is interesting that in both he is honest enough to depict that process. Fishke, with his limp and his speech impediment, does have powerful feelings; and he is downtrodden only because other people share Mendele's original attitude. Just as Mendele learns to have compassion for all Jews, so mankind must learn to have compassion for all human beings, even for Jews.

This point is reinforced near the beginning of Fishke's story: when Fishke describes himself and his wife—the lame leading the blind—he uses the term "foot beggars," remarking that beggars can be divided into numerous classifications. This leads Mendele to interrupt Fishke's story with a long descriptive catalogue of beggars, including foot beggars, van beggars, city beggars, field beggars, and starvelings of various sorts. And in spite of Alter's objections, he goes on to mention " 'pilgrims to Jerusalem, Jews on their way back from Jerusalem, Jews who were burned out, sick Jews, Jews with hemorrhoids and doctors' letters to prove it, deserted wives, widows of all sorts, writers, and—the devil won't take us, Reb Alter—we might as well include book peddlers.' " Finally Alter, who is basically impatient, can take no more and cuts Mendele off: " 'As far as I'm concerned, you can cut the whole story short: all of Israel—one big pauper' " (112). As Alter's remark indicates, the

poor Jews stand to the rest of the Jews as the Jews in general stand
to the rest of the world—they are outcasts, frowned upon and
humiliated for no good reason, dependent on everyone else's good-
will but usually disappointed in their expectations. Mendele even
finds that he can tell jokes about some of the beggars. One beggar,
for instance, was invited to the pauper's meal when a rich man's
daughter was married; but when he arrived, he had brought a guest
along. " 'Uncle,' " they asked him, " 'how is it that you brought
along another mouth to feed?' " " 'Oh,' he answered, 'that's my
son-in-law. I give him room and board!' " (114). Certainly the beggar has a lot of nerve; but on the other hand, when we consider how
the rich men in Abramovitsh's novels got rich, we are justified,
perhaps, in sympathizing with the beggar, though Mendele merely
finds him amusing.

Throughout Fishke's story, Mendele vacillates between sympathy
and sarcasm. At one point, Fishke describes the way Bayleh once
talked in her sleep, in words that clearly recall Mendele's earlier
prayer: " 'Don't torture me! What have I done to you? What do you
want from me? Don't ruin my life! What have I done to you?' "
Suddenly Fishke realizes how eloquent he has become in describing
his feelings about Bayleh and he becomes embarrassed; and Mendele launches into a digression in which he discusses the ways that
even the dullest people can be inspired, can say things they never
thought themselves capable of. This leads him to think of Balaam's
ass and to compare Fishke to an incompetent preacher who suddenly has an inspiration. "As soon as the moment of inspiration
evaporates, the ass remains an ass and the preacher, pardon the
comparison, a bag of wind and . . . but that's not my point." Of
course, it is his point; and what he again implies is that Fishke is less
than human, hardly capable even of using language. He pushes this
thought even further when he refers to Fishke as his "Golem," a
legendary Jewish figure made of clay and endowed with life by the
use of certain magic words, though, as he says, "the magic words I
was going to use to waken my Golem . . . would be about the
hunchbacked girl." The irony here is that the Golem was originally
created to defend the Jews from the onslaughts of their enemies,
while in this case, Fishke will be the instrument through which
Mendele will learn of his own oppressive tendencies. This process
begins almost immediately, for in order to provoke Fishke, Mendele begins an impassioned speech, reminiscent of Fishke's recent

words, in which he deplores the fate of innocent children who suffer because of their parents' sins. As he begins the sentence, "Some of these fine parents even remarry—," he suddenly realizes that Alter is sitting there and his criticism "fitted his position all too well. I had probably cut him to the quick. . . . I promised myself to be more careful in the future, to think twice before speaking once . . ." (141–44). It seems that Mendele has learned his lesson, that he must be careful about the way he treats those around him, that Alter and especially Fishke are not there simply to entertain him.

Nevertheless, just a few pages later—as Fishke describes the relationship that developed between Bayleh and himself and becomes so upset that he stops talking for a minute—Mendele tells us, "To make him talk again, I decided to tease him a little and said: 'You know, Fishke, you haven't even told us whether your hunchback is a pretty girl or not. Really, what can a hunchbacked girl have that makes her so attractive?' " (151). Mendele's cruelty in teasing Fishke, his reference to "your hunchback," and his question about her beauty all indicate a kind of callousness—cruelty, even—that makes us wonder about his earlier despair and the sincerity of his feelings. Mendele, at this point, is a most unattractive figure, having gone through so much himself, having classified himself as a beggar, and yet feeling himself superior to Fishke.

Fortunately, as Fishke continues his story, Mendele begins to find himself deeply moved, and at the end, when he realizes that Alter is Bayleh's father, he says, "By now everything was crystal clear to me and I sat there as if I had been doused with a pail of cold water" (215). His laughter and cynicism have disappeared, as Fishke's story suddenly intrudes on real life, as Alter sits there crying and beating his breast, lamenting, " 'I have sinned! I have ruined her life!' " Mendele becomes kindness itself: "I began to reassure Reb Alter for pity's sake. I tried to soothe him and minimize his sins: he was, after all, no more than flesh and blood" (215).[13] He is no longer playing a game, no longer having a good laugh or a little entertainment on his way to Glupsk. He is, instead, directly involved in the tragedy, and all he can feel is pity, both for Alter and for Fishke. And just as Fishke's story, this day's entertainment, has become real, so the whole novel—the squalor, the harshness, the despair—is also reality. Abramovitsh's novels are not simple entertainment, and anyone who regards them as such is making the same mistake as Mendele in his most cynical moments.

There is one last interchange that is important for illustrating Mendele's role in the novel. When Fishke has finished his story, Mendele tries to cheer him by saying

"Stop worrying, Fishke. We must never forget our beloved God. He can help us."

"I only want to ask you one question, Reb Mendele!" Fishke exclaimed bitterly. "Why did He have to bring us together again, her and me, and then separate us so suddenly? Why did our luck suddenly smile on us only to make things blacker than ever before? It's almost like spite work! Oh, Lord of Nations, whom hast Thou punished? Two unfortunate, miserable cripples, who would have been far better off if they'd never been born! Their lives have been so bleak, so full of pain and torments!"

I made a pious face, shook my head and said: "*Ta, ta ta!* You mustn't talk like that." I did not say this because it answered Fishke's cry of woe in any way, but rather because it has become a custom in the world. When misery forces someone to start asking embarrassing questions, you must chide him and slow him down with at least a "*ta, ta, ta!*" (213)

Suddenly we are back in the inn with Mendele, as he cries out to God. Here Fishke asks the same questions, and Mendele can only respond, "*Ta, ta, ta,*" just as in *Catch-22* Yossarian can find no words for the dying Snowden other than, "There, there."[14] Mendele has had his mystical moment, his Joblike encounter with the mysteries of God's ways, but it was a private moment. He is taken aback when Fishke verbalizes his thoughts, questions God's ways, and challenges God's wisdom; and he truly does not know how to answer. So he gives the traditional answer—which is no answer at all—then immediately reverts to learning how they can recover Bayleh. As Abramovitsh has shown us in the earlier works, these metaphysical questions are interesting, but what the people need is action; and Mendele moves right into action. Nevertheless, he has discovered that he and Fishke share a close relationship, that Fishke's troubles and questions are the same as his own, so that he ends the book by announcing "that two new Jews have arrived in the city of Glupsk!" (216). No longer are they Mendele and his Golem, sophisticated Mendele and tongue-tied, lame Fishke. They are two Jews, two human beings.

This rather lengthy examination of Mendele's role in the novel is necessitated by his importance for the general themes of the book. Mendele in *Fishke* is the most well-rounded of Abramovitsh's characters. He is a complex human being responding to the complex pressures that a Jew faced in his time. Like Alter, he is "no more than flesh and blood," but if we understand his relationship to Fishke's story and the implications of his learning experience, we will have a better understanding of our relationship to Abramovitsh's most powerful novels.

IV Fishke

The parallels and contrasts between the two halves of *Fishke,* the frame story and Fishke's story, are of the greatest importance, for, as we have just seen, the two halves finally come together, interpenetrate. Fishke and Mendele are parallel characters who are forced to learn something about themselves and who end up asking the same eternal questions. Fishke may not have Mendele's facility with words, but his feelings are as deep, his reactions to the brutalities of his life are as affecting as Mendele's. The picture of Fishke pouring out his heart to the two booksellers, searching for words, trying to describe feelings that he never knew he had—that the world tried to prevent him from having—is quite simply pathetic, just as Mendele is pathetic in front of the Russian official or at the inn. Isaac Bashevis Singer has said, "The Yiddish tradition, in my mind, is a tradition of sentimentality and of social justice,"[15] and though Singer rejects this tradition (referring to the sentimental aspects as "schmaltz"), there can be no question that these are two of the pillars on which *Fishke* stands. We shall soon examine the question of social justice in more detail, though we have already touched on it, but the sense of pathos runs throughout. Though we see it most in Fishke and Mendele, it also appears in Alter, Bayleh, and numerous other characters. Abramovitsh does not get quite so carried away as a Dreiser or a Dickens, but as a social reformer, his use of pathos is an important tool. It may well be that only a person with a heart of stone could read about Little Nell's death without laughing, as Oscar Wilde said; but Dickens was reflecting the brutal, harsh world in which his characters lived, and it is hardly possible to issue an effective call for social justice without somehow describing the pathos that injustice creates. *Fishke* may, at first, look like one of the old melodramatic novels by Sue, with its use of the underworld, its sudden discovery of familial relationships (Mendele and Chaya-Traina, Alter and Bayleh), its panoramic view of society,[16] and the sense of pathos that underlies the whole fabric;

but it is a matter of fact that the Jews' situation was indeed pathetic. We have already seen this in Mendele's relationship with the outside world. Fishke's story parallels Mendele's by dealing with the brutalities and injustices within the Jewish world.

The question of social justice is a bit more complex in *Fishke* than it might at first seem (and we must remember that Abramovitsh's descriptions of the beggars is based on his own youthful experiences with Abraham the Lame). There is, for example, one outstanding speech that seems to summarize all of Abramovitsh's previous criticism of the rich in his earlier novels: /

Why should the rich sit around like princes, doing nothing, while others work for them? Doesn't everything they own come from other people's toil, other people's tears and sweat? They think they're fine folks. They take care of themselves and want others to work. A rich man, the fatter he is and the bigger his belly, the more honor and respect he gets. With us it's just the opposite. A healthy beggar has to be ashamed and hide like a thief. Otherwise people raise a hue and cry and demand why such a healthy fellow isn't working. It's time for a change—let the rich try to work a bit! What's wrong with them? They're not sick. (115–16)

Strangely enough, this speech is delivered not by Fishke but by Feibush, the novel's nearest approach to an actual villain. Feibush's response to the injustices of society has been to become, as Fishke repeatedly calls him, a "bastard." He and his band "set great store on the knack of putting on an act. . . . Whenever it paid, these fine folks could become hunchbacked, blind, deaf or dumb, or lame" (122). Their creed, as Feibush explains it, is that if people " 'won't give you alms with good will, you have to get it out of them with tricks. . . . What does the Rabbi, or the judge, or any of that pack of officials do? They all disguise themselves and perform tricks' " (117). This description of the rabbi recalls Mendele's suspicions in *Dos Kleyne Mentshele*, and the reference to performing tricks relates directly to the career of Yitzchok-Avrom.

Fishke, on the other hand " 'often defended the rich and stood up for their honor' " (122). In this he foreshadows Peretz's Bontsha the Silent, who is about to be rewarded in heaven for having never complained on earth, though he was one of the worst-treated people who ever lived. When asked what he wants as his reward, all he can think of is a hot roll with butter, at which "the judge and the angels bend their heads in shame at this unending meekness they have created on earth."[17] How, we wonder, could Fishke defend the rich and stand up for their honor when, as we have seen over and over in Abramovitsh's novels, the rich have no honor? This line of reasoning, however, leads us to Feibush's response, which we must reject; Fishke recalls the one time he *was* tempted to take Feibush's course. As he recalls a conversation he had with another bathhouse attendant, he gives us an interesting picture of his internal debate: " 'Shmerl's words awakened the little devil who sleeps in the breast of each of us sinners. The little devil in mine awoke with a biting laugh, pricked my heart, confused my mind, stirring up old insults and injuries which were buried there and gathering dust' " (163). Fishke is not insensible to the injustices of the rich and to the horrors of the poorhouse, but he knows that his feeling for revenge—Feibush's creed—comes from the devil. He knows that Feibush is not campaigning for social justice but is simply trying to enrich himself; and we know, as we watch Feibush woo Fishke's wife, that if Feibush were rich, he would be among the worst of the bloodsuckers. He represents the type of social reformer who calls for social reform only to excuse his own crimes, and while his condemnation of the rich is justified, the thought that lies behind it is not. Fishke may be naive; Feibush is evil.

But while Abramovitsh shows us Feibush and other charlatans, while he shows us again the numerous evils from which his characters suffer and calls again for social justice, he also shows us the beauty and depth of feeling that can exist even in the lowest classes of society. The whole description of Fishke's relationship with Bayleh introduces a beauty, a tenderness that we have not seen before in Abramovitsh's work. It is a real romance, in spite of Miron's parenthetical questioning "whether we can use the word 'romantic' to designate the love between a cripple and a hunchback."[18] Of course we can—this is one of the main points of the book; it is one of the things that Mendele learns and it is one of the things that the reader must learn. If a broken-down old nag deserves respect, how much more do Fishke and Bayleh deserve it! And while Fishke's situation stems indirectly from the external persecutions of the Jewish people, he is equally the victim of internal injustice. The whole concept of "cholera grooms" betrays the attitude that the lowest members of society have no feelings—and Fishke was even passed over in the choice of "cholera grooms." But when he describes his feelings for Bayleh, the kind of brotherly love and

the outrage he feels over her misfortunes, we get a glimpse of the
inner Fishke, of the Fishke whose body is buried in mud but whose
forehead touches heaven: " 'I looked at her. Tears were rolling
down her cheeks. Her face was aflame. She looked at me and smiled
sadly. That look of hers took the strength out of me. My heart
stopped beating and there was a pounding in my temples. I didn't
know what happened to me and . . . before I knew what I was
saying, the words escaped from my mouth: "My dear soul!' "
(150). Like Mendele at the inn, Fishke reveals himself; and we
realize that we are not dealing with a Bontsha or with a Golem but
with a sensient and sensitive human being. That is why, at the end,
when Fishke questions God's ways, we are at an even higher level of
consciousness than we were when Mendele asked the same questions.

Isaiah Rabinovich criticizes Abramovitsh's use of the beggars in
Fishke because Abramovitsh does not show "the psychological world
bubbling and fermenting within each one of them,"[19] but all this
means is that Abramovitsh did not write the novel that Rabinovich
thinks he should have written, an in-depth study of the beggar class.
Actually we do receive a complex portrait of Fishke, who is not
simply the beggar with a heart of gold but one who suffers and yet
rises above his suffering, who questions and yet believes, who is
debased and yet noble. Our attitude—and Mendele's attitude—
toward Fishke implies a great deal about our attitude toward other
people, and it is significant that the novel ends on a note of reconciliation, of coming together: Mendele finds a common bond between himself and Fishke.

V *Marriage*

The novel's great symbol for this coming together and for solidarity is marriage. Miron says that the major theme of *Fishke* is "the
callous dehumanization of sex and marriage in contemporary Jewish
life."[20] Certainly this particular kind of dehumanization existed and
may be one of the novel's themes, but to cite it as the novel's major
theme makes the novel far too narrow. Marriage, in the novel,
operates on a higher plane. At one point, Mendele mentions in
passing the *Song of Songs.* The single reference should not be
pushed too far, but it is worth noting that this great biblical song of
love and marriage was interpreted by Jewish commentators as an
allegorical description of the relationship between God and the

Jews.[21] Marriage was also used as a symbol for this relationship by a number of prophets, perhaps most strikingly by Hosea, who described his marriage to the wanton Gomer. It seems likely that Abramovitsh was relying on the traditional use of marriage as a symbol.

There are, in *Fishke*, four major marriages or prospective marriages: Alter's first marriage, which ended in divorce; Alter's unsuccessful attempt at matchmaking; Chaya-Traina's unsuccessful attempt to marry off her daughter to Mendele's son; and Fishke's marriage to the blind beggar. This list hardly constitutes what one might call a recommendation for the efficacy of marriage. Each item represents, to some extent, a disaster. Mendele shudders at the possibility of becoming Chaya-Traina's in-law, and besides, his son is only thirteen or fourteen. We cannot blame Chaya-Traina for trying—the lot of an unmarried female was indeed unenviable—but such marriages, however common they may have been, would not be likely to make either partner especially happy. Such a marriage was Fishke's. Two complete strangers were practically drafted into marrying each other to satisfy the desires of the wedding guests. This probably describes Alter's first marriage as well, which would explain his having divorced his wife and abandoned his children. Early in the novel Mendele asks Alter, "Why did you divorce your first wife and ruin her whole life? . . . What happened to your poor children by your first marriage? Do you know?" Alter can only answer " *'Beh!'* " Mendele understands that "Alter's last *'beh'* was a bitter one. Contrition, repentance, and self-accusation seemed to be wrapped up in it. Surely his mean treatment of his first wife and their children must have left a wound in his heart" (35–36). By the novel's end, we know that he feels remorse; but his actions have caused a great deal of suffering and grief for his ex-wife and for Bayleh. Finally, Alter's attempt to make a match between two daughterless families represents the absolute absurdity of the system. Of course this represents a dehumanization of marriage, but it also represents more, for marriage is intended to be a sacred joining together of people, and yet these marriages and prospective marriages end in fragmentation and disharmony.

Fragmentation and disharmony, however, pervade the novel. We have already examined Mendele's early relationship with Fishke, which seems to pit them against each other, but there are numerous other examples. One of the most striking occurs near the book's

beginning, when, before they recognize each other, Mendele and
Alter fight over who was responsible for getting them stuck in the
mud: "It must have looked strange, indeed: two Jewish champions
in their prayer shawls and *tefillin*, facing each other in a rage, ready
to exhibit their prowess and slap each other, right in the middle of
this open field, as though they'd been arguing in a *House of Study*,
forgive the comparison" (21). (It is important here to keep in mind
the essentially religious nature of the house of study, since "Jewish
tradition has always considered study of the Torah literature as a
mode of worship. . . ."[22]) Mendele's comparison is at first glance
humorous, but as we visualize two Jews dressed for prayer actually
ready to engage in physical combat and then hear that this is how
things are in the House of Study, we are entitled to be a bit horrified. They make no attempt to settle the problem rationally, to
discuss the problem peacefully and come up with a solution; and if
this is the condition in the House of Study, how much more so is it
the case throughout Jewish society!

It is no accident, then, that the novel begins on the seventeenth
of Tammuz and that Mendele refers so often to the Ninth of Ab.
Miron has shown how important nature is in Abramovitsh's work.[23]
His choice of dates is also important, for the action of *Fishke*—that
is, Mendele's introduction and Fishke's telling of his story—takes
place during the period that immediately precedes the day com-
memorating the destruction of the first and second Temples. There
is a Talmudic comment on these events that pertains here. The
Talmud says that the First Temple was destroyed because of three
sins—idolatry, immorality, and bloodshed—but that the Second
Temple was destroyed because there existed in Israel hatred without cause. This shows us, according to the Talmud, that, by itself,
groundless hatred equals the three sins. Again, it is not pushing too
far to see that groundless hatred implies a fragmented society, a
society that, though it may practice charitable deeds, is based on
disharmony. This is exactly what we see in *Fishke* over and over
again. The people have become dehumanized, the fabric of Jewish
society has been torn, and Abramovitsh uses marriage—or, more
precisely, unsuccessful marriage—as a symbol that the whole
people has failed to come together. As we saw earlier in this chapter, Abramovitsh supported Pinsker insofar as the latter called for
Jewish solidarity. So here in *Fishke der Krumer* he is calling for
solidarity, for the people to come together, to cease bickering—

whether in the house of study, in the road, or in discussions of political philosophy—and at least be strong within, so that they may arrive at some rational solutions to their problems. In short, he is calling on them to restore the symbolic marriage that should unite them. And, as in the prophets, if the people can come together, their symbolic marriage with God, the subject of Mendele's and Fishke's questions, will also be strengthened.

VI *Odessa*

To complicate the question, Abramovitsh moves us out of the small town milieu, to which we have become accustomed, into the big city, Odessa, where Fishke spends some time on his way back to Glupsk. This lengthy digression has its humorous side, but it is also quite serious. In it, Abramovitsh uses the ancient dichotomies between the city and the country, the naive bumpkin and the sophisticated city dweller, to illustrate just how far apart many Jews are. Fishke can only view Odessa through Glupskian eyes, and consequently everything looks strange, for Odessa was in the forefront of the Russian Haskala. Even the Russians called it "our little Paris," and the Jews played a big part in building it up.[24] What we have, then, as Miron points out, is a strong contrast between Odessa and the Haskala, on the one hand, and Glupsk, with its mass of unenlightened Jews almost untouched by modern learning, on the other.

The first person Fishke meets in Odessa is a young author, like Gutman in *Dos Kleyne Mentshele*, who is dressed like a German and who wanders from house to house trying to sell his books, always unsuccessfully. Fishke, however, who follows him around, asks at each house for a handout, and always comes away with at least a few groschen. Fishke assumes that the young Maskil is just another kind of beggar, and, in a very funny conversation, tries to talk to him; but the Maskil uses many Hebraic words in his Yiddish, words that Fishke thinks are German, and their conversation remains a series of misunderstandings. Finally the young man just runs away.

Actually, Fishke's misunderstandings, like everything else in the novel, make some important points. For example, when the Maskil asks him if he is an author, Fishke thinks he is being asked if he is a beggar. Of course Fishke is here being satirized for his Glupskian ignorance; but the Maskil is also being satirized, because in actuality he *is* a beggar. In addition, the society of Odessa is being satirized, since even the men who are shaven, a sure sign of modern thinking, throw the poor Maskil out of their houses, refusing to buy his books. They are willing to give charity to Fishke, but not to support the Maskil's work, the work of education and modernization.

Later, as Fishke walks down the street with his friend Yontl, he deplores what he sees in Odessa: " 'Just look at the men holding the ladies' hands! It's a sin just to look! Jews with shaven faces! Jewish women with their own hair—sweeping the street with their long trailing dresses which are cut so low in front that you can see their bosoms. *Feh*, it's disgusting. . . . *Ach*, if we could bring our Jews from Glupsk here! Then this would be a city, a Jewish city, with Jewish customs . . .' " (188). To an extent Fishke is right, since modernization and assimilation so often led to apostasy and conversion. And yet we also know that he is wrong, for we have repeatedly been shown the deficiencies of Glupsk and the other *shtetls* and the way of life that they represent. These deficiencies are evident in Fishke's description of the bathhouses in the two cities: " 'In the Glupsk bathhouse, the water had a different taste, a different color, and was somehow soupier than other water. You knew right away that this was a Jewish bathhouse. But here in Odessa? The water was fresh and clear, just plain water, like water should be—drinking water' " (195).

The most interesting episode in Odessa occurs again as Fishke and Yontl wander the streets. Once, "two well-dressed gentlemen came towards us, Frenchmen, and Yontl stretched out his hand. One of them stopped to talk to him for a minute and gave him some money." When Yontl tells Fishke that this man is the chief teacher in the Jewish school, Fishke cannot control himself:

" 'May all my enemies look like that!' I spat. 'From the looks of my handsome *melamed* [teacher], I can imagine your so-called *Talmud-Torah* here. I ask you, Yontl, aren't you ashamed of yourself to say that this is good? . . . Look at him and look at our Reb Hertzele Mazik in Glupsk, God forgive the comparison. There is a Jew for you! Why, all of Glupsk is full of Reb Hertzele Mazik. Who extols the dead at a funeral? He! Who recites psalms for the dead at the cemetery? He, again! When he goes from house to house every week to collect his fee for teaching the children, folks carry the money toward him! On *Simches-Torah* he runs to the wealthy houses with the little boys from the *Talmud-Torah* to say prayers in honor of the rich. When he cries, 'Holy sheep!' the little boys answer, 'Baa, ba-a-a!' It's something to see. And your Frenchman? What would he look like extolling the dead at a funeral or saying prayers in honor of the rich?' " (189).

Of course, this Frenchified teacher is none other than Abramovitsh himself. As Miron points out, this passage is another jab at the Glupskian way of seeing things, but it also raises questions about Abramovitsh's way of life. "The question posed by Fishke—which remains, significantly, unanswered—is what kind of education can such a 'Frenchified' Odessa gentleman give to his scholars. Certainly not the authentic Jewish one. . . ."[25] Miron goes on to say that "Fishke does not, and never will, comprehend the world of his 'Frenchified' creator. Nothing, as far as he is concerned, could be more remote and meaningless than the language, concepts, and values of this world." Mendele is the mediator between Fishke and Abramovitsh: not only does he understand both worlds, but he actually converts Fishke's speech into a language that we readers can understand.[26] In addition to the important points that Miron makes about this passage, it is worth noting that the passage reinforces what we have already seen in the novel: the need for unity, for solidarity, for a Mendele who can somehow bring together the worlds of Glupsk and Odessa. Mendele has been a kind of mediator throughout Abramovitsh's works, a mouthpiece through whom Abramovitsh could address the people. Now his role goes even further, as he becomes a symbol uniting the simple folk of Israel, represented by Fishke, and the sophisticated Maskilim, represented by Abramovitsh "the Frenchman."

VII   Fishke der Krumer: *Conclusion*

In the letter in which he dedicated *Fishke der Krumer* to his friend Menasha Margolis, Abramovitsh wrote that

it has been my lot to descend to the depths, to the cellars of our Jewish life. My stock in trade is: rags and moldy wares. My dealings are with paupers and beggars, the poor wretches of life; with degenerates, cripples, charlatans and other unfortunates, the dregs of humanity. I always dream of beggars. Before my eyes, I always see a basket soaring—the old, familiar Jewish beggar basket. No matter which way I turn my eyes, the basket is before me. No matter what I say or do, the basket comes soaring up to me! *Oy*, it's always the basket, the Jewish beggar basket! (15)

Fishke, perhaps Abramovitsh's most accomplished work, still involves his favorite subject, the plight of the Jews in nineteenth century Eastern Europe, especially the poorer classes of Jews, whom he portrays with a vivid realism. As Joshua Rothenberg says, "He concentrated his literary material on that which he found necessary for his social mission and on that which was sharp enough and colorful enough for his artistic sense and taste."[27] The novel is didactic, for Abramovitsh never forgot his social mission, but it is also his best structured work. He has abandoned the looseness of the real picaresque or Quixotic fiction in his masterful use of the frame story and Fishke's story, as they gradually intertwine. The characters of *Fishke* are also among his best-drawn creations, from Alter, Fishke, and Mendele to even so minor a character as Chaya-Traina. Finally, it is one of his most touching works. In *Benjamin the Third* we are touched when Benjamin and Senderel are imprisoned, but the overt satire, the sense of caricature, stands between us and the work. In *Fishke*, however, the tone has changed; and the work, while it is honest and shows the bad as well as the good, engages our sympathy rather than our humor or even our sense of outrage, as the earlier, more satiric works did. The problem is still "the basket, the Jewish beggar basket," but it is also, "How can the meaning of that basket best be conveyed and what can be done about it?" Abramovitsh's answer to the latter question may not be fully satisfactory in its vagueness, but the question, at least, is stated with painful clarity.

CHAPTER 7

Dos Vintshfingerl
A Time to Seek and a Time to Lose

I   Dos Vintshfingerl

Fishke der Frumer was Abramovitsh's masterpiece. His last, longest, and most ambitious novel, *Dos Vintshfingerl (The Magic Wishing Ring)*, is a great comedown, in some ways a most disappointing work, although he wrote to his friend Binshtok that "it will be, in some respects, the greatest of all my works."[1] The reasons for the novel's failure are many and complex, and can be seen at least partially in the novel's history. The first version, which appeared in 1865, was a long and rather unsuccessful short story. A new version began to appear as a serialized novel in Sholem Aleichem's *Yidishe Folks-Biblyotek* in 1888. This version consisted of an important prologue and the beginnings of a long novel in which Abramovitsh planned to present ". . . Jewish life and the most important matters which come before us. I will detail the Jewish situation and show what we must do to better it."[2] This project proved to be bigger than Abramovitsh had suspected, however, and he worked at it for more than twenty years. Finally, in 1909, a set of his complete works began to appear and he quickly brought to a close the essentially unfinished novel, partly by tying up some loose ends and by transforming the 1888 prologue into an epilogue.[3] In the present discussion we will be examining the final version of the novel, in spite of its flaws, simply because it is worth seeing what Abramovitsh finally decided on. (As usual, the novel also exists in a Hebrew version, *Be'emek Habacha [In the Vale of Tears]*, which is essentially the same as the Yiddish.)

The novel divides into three distinct sections. The first half adheres to Abramovitsh's original plan of an epic overview of Jewish life in Eastern Europe. In the second section, the novel turns into a melodramatic potboiler in the tradition of Eugène Sue. The last part

135

of the novel becomes a didactic—even propagandistic—examination of the Haskala in the light of recent Jewish history and almost an apologia for Abramovitsh's role in the movement. The novel opens with a description of the hero Hershele's hometown, the *shtetl* of Kabtsansk (Pauperville). In the novel's opening chapters we see the poverty and degradation of life in Kabtsansk, and we see Hershele as a little boy intrigued by such wonders as a modern doctor who visits the town and captivated by such magical stories as the one about a magic wishing ring, a kind of Jewish ring of the Nibelungen, which gives its owners the power to receive everything they ask for. In fact the Kabtsanskers, like their brethren in Tuneyadevka, spend all their time wishing for things as a result of their total poverty. After many youthful adventures, Hershele travels with his father to Glupsk, which by now has become a big city, in order to accompany him in his yearly task of leading High Holiday prayers. There he spends his spare time studying Talmud in a small study house, where he becomes friendly with Reb Abraham and with Moshele, a boy his own age whose family is also very poor. Soon, however, his father sickens and, leaving the boy in Reb Abraham's care, returns to Kabtsansk, where he dies. After a complex—and melo-dramatic—series of events, Hershele helps his childhood sweet-heart (an unheard of thing among Jews of this time) Bayleh find a job and Moshele is kidnapped by a pair of *khappers*.

At this point, the story concentrates on Bayleh, for the woman who ostensibly hired her as a serving girl has actually kidnapped her and taken her to a brothel, from which she escapes many pages later with the help of Raphael, a young Maskil who has befriended Hershele. Raphael, meanwhile, has fallen in love with Chintze, the married daughter of one of his business associates. Chintze, who becomes infected with Haskala thought, also loves Raphael and despises her ultraorthodox husband, though he later becomes a Maskil and divorces her. Many of the loose ends are drawn together when Raphael goes to Leipzig and sends for Hershele and Chintze. Raphael and Chintze are married against her parents' will, and Hershele has left the backward world from which he came, including Bayleh, who has returned to Kabtsansk, and moved to one of the centers of the Haskala. Moshele, in turn, has been rescued by a rich Maskil and almost immediately becomes a Maskil himself. The story ends as he tells his parents, who have benefited from the rich man's largesse, that he will be a doctor.

The epilogue takes place many years later, after the pogroms, as the people of Kabtsansk are gathered in the cemetery to mourn the victims of official Russian anti-Semitism. A rich man, dressed in modern German style, appears. The people are afraid of him until he speaks to them in Yiddish, asking where certain graves are. This is Hershele, a modern, assimilated Jew, calling himself Heinrich Cohen, who has been sent by a commission of German Jews to assess the effects of the pogroms. After visiting his parents' graves and learning that Bayleh has been raped and killed in the pogroms, he goes into town where he meets Mendele, whom he had already met in Tuneyadevka and to whom he expresses his feelings of solidarity with the Russian Jews: " 'I am a son of the people, a Jew like all my ancestors, fathers and forefathers.' "[4] As Miron says, "These words, rather than recording reality, are expressions of a fervent wish, a wish involving an implicit self-criticism. Hershele's desire to belong to the world of 'the Jew' implies a bitter disillusionment with the influences which separated him from it in the first place, i.e., with the *Haskala* and its literature."[5]

If most of the story sounds silly, the reason is probably because it is silly, full of kidnappings, tears, last minute escapes, sudden conversions to the Haskala, and a number of other melodramatic devices, many of which make the novel sound like a Yiddish *Mysteries of Paris*. Abramovitsh even adopts Sue's habit of giving nicknames to his underworld characters like the Turk or Auntie Shaintze. Sue, of course, filled his novels with brief passages of social criticism, something that influenced Abramovitsh throughout his career, but the social criticism of *Dos Vintshfingerl* is extremely weak. In fact, this may be largely due to Mendele's absence from the final version until the last few pages. *Dos Vintshfingerl* has none of the subtlety and irony of the earlier works, and the social criticism falls flat. For the most part the novel lacks that combination of bitter satire and love for the people that characterizes Abramovitsh's best works. The characters are too much like stick figures whom the author pushes wherever he wants, and the omniscient narrator is almost colorless.

Finally, especially toward the end, the novel gives the impression that Abramovitsh was foundering, that he knew the book was not artistically very good but that he did not know exactly how to improve it and consequently sought easy solutions. This statement, however, must be confined to the aesthetic aspects of the novel, for in terms of the novel's ideas, it is indeed a complex work, showing

Abramovitsh's own uncertainties about what had taken place in Jewish life and in his own life during the previous fifty years. One of the reasons that the novel seems so confusing at the end is that Abramovitsh was himself confused, that he increasingly recognized the ambiguous nature of his own position. Previously this ambiguity had appeared most forcefully in *Fishke,* in the scene where Fishke saw Abramovitsh walking down the street in Odessa. In that work Abramovitsh seemed to resolve the problem of his own place in Jewish life, but he knew that that resolution was insufficient because it was too idealistic, too impractical. Miron points out that Abramovitsh would have been just as out of place in Kabtsansk as Hershele was.[6]

The essential problem for Abramovitsh was that since the beginning of his career, and in spite of all his satiric criticism, he had been firmly committed to the Haskala. And yet, as historical events, especially the pogroms, had shown, the Haskala was in large part a failure. Its adherents tended to be cut off from the Jewish masses, it created new divisions among the Jewish people, and it did nothing to stave off the pogroms. To the anti-Semites, a Jew was a Jew, whether he wore traditional clothing and sidecurls or the most current fashions. One result of the pogroms, as we saw earlier, was the rise of Jewish nationalism. Dispirited Maskilim turned to nationalism as the new movement that would save the Jews. Abramovitsh sympathized with the nationalists, certainly, and some of their thought is reflected in *Fishke,* but he never really joined them, never abandoned the Haskala, as they did. Still, he was clearly shaken by what had happened. It is ironic that in the epilogue Hershele, the Maskil, says, " 'All my earlier ideas have been destroyed, like a sunken ship, by what I have seen in the last few weeks,' " and Mendele, who at least seems like a traditional Jew, responds, " 'Still, we must not lose hope,' I told him, trying to offer some consolation, according to custom."[7] This is a far cry from the "Ta, ta, ta" that he offered to Fishke. It is the consolation of a man who has lived through the pogroms offered to a man who is almost entirely cut off from the mass of Jews but who wants to feel that he is one of them. Hershele certainly does not represent Abramovitsh in the novel, but their situations are much alike; and the question that Abramovitsh seems to have been struggling with was whether the Haskala was nothing more than a *vintshfingerl,* a magic wishing ring that he and his generation saw as a means of providing all the good things in life but that actually cut them off from their fellow Jews. Were he and his colleagues like the citizens of Kabtsansk, ignoring reality and wasting their time on idle wishing?

Abramovitsh agonizes over this problem throughout the novel, especially toward the end. Early in the book he provides one easy resolution that he later seems to reject. When we first meet Raphael, Abramovitsh makes an important distinction between the early "concealed Maskilim" and the modern sort. The early ones, "may they rest in peace, were not sundered from the rest of the Jews, neither in their religious practices nor in their dress; they studied the Law, they prayed thrice daily, they washed before and said grace after meals like everyone else. . . . They did everything like everyone else, except that . . . they shortened their capotes a bit . . . they shortened their sidecurls . . . and they combed out their beards, all of which caused consternation in the Jewish world." These people, he tells us, "were the new saviors in education. They looked like ordinary people, their mouths closed, not babbling; but Holy God what was going on in their hearts! Their Judaism glowed in their hearts, burned like a holy fire from love for the whole world. They dreamed of the beginning of a new, beautiful world. They hoped it would soon emerge, in a brighter day—it would be a Paradise. They were a close group . . . but instead of liquor they drank in the words of the holy prophets, of well-written books. . . ." They were also eager to educate anyone who wanted to learn and gave unselfishly of their time. These dedicated people, he says, "didn't know even what our modern precocious children know, that the secret of the Haskala is without doubt an open mouth, and fervor, bellowing, a heart cold as ice; they didn't know that the best Torah is business, and the best language is money . . ." (XI, 160–61). In a sense we are back in *Ha'avot Vehabanim*, except that the roles have been reversed. Now the sons are wrong, for they have abandoned the principles and ethics of the fathers, those fathers who forty or fifty years earlier were rebellious sons themselves. The generations have changed again, and while Abramovitsh played a leading part in the earlier change, he is now troubled that change continues. This is, of course, a familiar pattern: a revolutionary generation often deplores the way the next generation continues the revolution.

Nevertheless, Abramovitsh realized that this solution was too simplistic. He could not defend his whole life's work on the basis of early Haskala ideals and blame the failure of those ideals on the new generation. Later on in the novel he gives a more balanced picture of the earlier generation, showing their faults as well as their virtues. That he thought such a picture was necessary is emphasized by the way this long description is inserted in the story, totally out of place and incongruous. In a passage that sounds a great deal like an apologia, we are told that

We must not so easily dismiss the Maskilim of the earlier generation. We must consider the time and place in which they lived. You might also keep in mind that if it had not been for them, we would not have our modern scholars. . . . When the door from the House of Study to the Haskala opened a little, the Jews let themselves madly sneak through. But how can one justify people today, for whom the door to the Haskala has never been closed? The early ones were misled unwillingly, unknowingly, but today people are misled knowingly. . . .

And you, wise men of the new generation, don't touch on the honor of the previous generation's wise men just because [they didn't get involved in the same kind of quarrels as you]. In the course of time, new thoughts and new needs will arise for your children after you. Perhaps your children will then laugh at their fathers, at their theories and their dreams. Every age brings forth new birds. New birds—new songs! . . . (XII, 367–68)

There is real agony in these words, a plea on behalf of the early Maskilim, who tried as hard as they could and who deserved more than a casual dismissal, let alone scorn. Perhaps they were misled, but they were misled with the best of intentions. They did not intend, according to Abramovitsh, to rend the fabric of Jewish life; they wanted to improve Jewish life. Nevertheless, when he says that the Haskala "moved like a plague, striking the Jew unexpectedly" (XII, 401), we must see the simile as more than just a figure of speech. The Haskala did indeed reach epidemic proportions, but the Maskilim would hardly have referred to themselves as carriers of a plague. Still, as we saw in *Ha'avot Vehabanim* and as we see in *Dos Vintshfingerl*, the Haskala caused rifts even within families ("One has only to check the records of the time to see for sure that there had never before been so many divorces among Jews" [XI, 188]) let alone within the whole community. Now, with the Haskala in disgrace even among its own supporters, Abramovitsh was being forced to reexamine his whole life's work; and what he found, more and more, was that he was cut off from the Jewish masses, that, like

Hershele, he could not go home again—except through the figure of Mendele.

And yet he could not admit that his life was a failure, as indeed it was not, for the Haskala had been a necessary movement and had accomplished a great deal. At the very least, it had publicized the plight of the Jews and raised Jewish self-consciousness; and Abramovitsh, of course, played a leading part in this aspect of the movement. What Abramovitsh sensed was that as a result of the Haskala and the recent pogroms, Jewish life was entering a new stage, and what Miron says about the 1888 prologue applies to the whole work: *Dos Vintshfingerl,* "is a comment on the crisis of Jewish culture in modern times and it is a very personal and self-searching comment."[8] While Abramovitsh was desperately defending the heroes and ideals of his generation, he was also raising questions that are still pertinent. What, for example, is the relationship between the modern assimilated Jew and his Jewish background? What is the relationship between him and the rest of the world? How does the outside world regard the assimilated Jew? As the pogroms had shown (and as Hitler was to show even more forcefully), no matter how assimilated a Jew may have been, he was still a Jew. Was the proper response, therefore, to abandon any attempt at assimilation?

All of these problems—assimilation, Jewish nationalism, the success or failure of the Haskala—contain infinite complexities that still have not been worked out. It is not surprising, therefore, that Abramovitsh found them puzzling. What happened, though, is that he began *Dos Vintshfingerl,* in epic terms and found himself overwhelmed by the complexities of the issues he was raising. His perplexity is evident in the novel's confused, haphazard construction as well as in its reliance on melodrama, cliche,[9] tepid social criticism, and themes that had already appeared many times in his works. In short, the novel has numerous aesthetic drawbacks, but mirrors in the most significant ways Abramovitsh's own doubts and hopes about Jewish existence. If the Yiddish title expresses the doubt that the Haskala may have been nothing more than a wishing ring, the Hebrew title offers the same hopeful idea that Mendele expresses to Hershele. At first glance, *In the Vale of Tears* seems to be another indication of despair, but actually the phrase occurs at least twice in important religious texts, and both times it has positive implications. In Psalm 84, for example, the poet describes pilgrims on their way to the Temple in Jerusalem: "Passing through the valley of weeping *(be'emek habacha)* they make it a place of springs."[10] This psalm, following a series that express despair over the sufferings of the Jews, injects a hopeful note, as the vale of tears becomes a fertile valley. Similarly, in the poem "Lecha Dodi," which is used in Friday evening prayers to welcome the Sabbath, there is a passage that reads, "Shrine of the King, royal city, arise! Come forth from thy ruins. Long enough have you dwelt in the vale of tears! He will show you abundant mercy."[11] Certainly this passage is very closely related to Mendele's words of comfort, and clearly Abramovitsh, whatever doubts and fears he had about the past and the future, was confident that the Jewish people at least had a future. As in *Benjamin the Third,* we see the problems and horrors that the Jews had to face, but we know that they will endure.

Two interesting passages in *Dos Vintshfingerl* illustrate, perhaps as well as anything else, the ambiguities that abound in the novel. Early in the book, the narrator bitterly describes the way the Kabtsanskers regard themselves. After telling us that they view Kabtsansk as the navel of the world (an interesting Homeric echo), the most important city on earth, he continues:

For them alone the sun shines during the day and the moon and stars at night. God devotes himself to them, He has nothing to do besides caring for his Kabtsansk Jews. . . . He makes it rain for their cattle and so their goats will have a pasture. . . . He makes a bountiful harvest of potatoes, onions, and garlic so that the Jews, poor things, will have enough to eat. All in all, the Guardian of Israel never sleeps—He works miracles, He keeps the world going just for them, just for them. . . . Therefore Jews blow the ram's horn, sing hymns and intone praises, therefore they make in His honor their noodle pudding on the Sabbath, matzo balls and pancakes on Passover, dance for all their worth on Simches Torah. On Chanukah they thank him with dreidels, on Purim with noisemakers, they dress up and put on Purim plays—the whole comedy in the name of Heaven, for His Holy Name's sake. . . . Truly they know of only one other city, which hovers always before their eyes, which abounds with legions of angels, winged officers and couriers from the Blessed Lord to the children of Israel—this is the holy city of Jerusalem, where Jews lie buried on the earth—in the holy earth of Israel—living corpses which don't putrify, which don't decay. . . . But alas, Jerusalem is today desolate . . . and for us, Jewish children, He exists in Kabtsansk—in Kabtsansk, in exile. (XI, 16–17)

The bitterness in this passage is startling, in its ironic praise of God, its mocking of religious celebrations, its despair over life in exile and over the Zionist dream of returning to Jerusalem. The passage offers no hope, no reasonable alternative. There seems to be not a single bright spot in Jewish existence, and the passage blasphemously makes God responsible.

This passage, however, is countered by another equally striking one later in the book. After we see the incredible poverty in which Moshele's family lives, we read the following:

On Friday nights, their hovel takes on a whole new appearance, washed and polished, clean in every corner. The table is covered with a white cloth and three polished brass candlesticks with the Sabbath candles, while the glow of two beautiful challas brushed with egg yolks catches the eye. A sweet stillness dominates the room, along with the smell of cooking food. . . . The mother, who all week was smeared and smudged, beams in her Sabbath kerchief; God's presence rests upon her. The barefoot girls, combed and shampooed, stay together in a corner, and you can see in their faces a look of joyful anticipation. . . .

The father and his son walk around the whole room singing the Sabbath song "Sholem Aleichem, Peace Be unto You!" This song concerns the holy angels, sent by God, the King of Kings, blessed be His name, who accompany the men home from the synagogue. The rag dealer is no longer the lowest of the low—he is a prince: he has a new soul and a new body. He says the blessings, washes, sits at the table, with his wife the princess and his children around him. . . . (XI, 121–22)

The passage, which continues at some length, presents exactly the opposite picture of what we have just seen. Not only is there no blasphemy here, but we are made to understand that the Sabbath, the religious ceremony, raises the people to a higher level of existence. Their lives are desperately hard, but they are sustained by the Sabbath. Here Abramovitsh denies that "spirituality has undermined our footing." Spirituality is one of the things that preserves the Jews in their most trying times.

What we see, then, is Abramovitsh both reproaching God for making the Jews' lives so hard and praising Him for giving them succor. As in his comments on the Haskala, Abramovitsh leaves us in an ambiguous position. The Jewish situation is both terrible and, in a way, beautiful. He offers us no reconciliation: both sides of the question contain a kind of truth and we are free to jump from one to the other. This latter passage contrasts also with a similar one in *Ha'avot Vehabanim*, but here, after the Haskala has proved less than fully successful, after the pogroms and horrors, he is more accusatory. The Sabbath is still beautiful, the Jews' spirituality is still important, but they deserve a better fate, they deserve more consideration from their God.

Dos Vintshfingerl is not a great work; it is not nearly so good as Abramovitsh's other novels. But it is important because it expresses in its very ambiguities the kind of immense problems, the kind of cosmic despair, the nationalist and religious feeling that filled the air in the late nineteenth century. That Abramovitsh could not resolve the problems simply indicates how great they were and how careful he was not to accept easy solutions. If we can overlook its absurdities, the novel leaves us at the same time with feelings of despair and feelings of hope.

II *Short Stories*

During the time that he was writing *Dos Vintshfingerl*, Abramovitsh also wrote a number of short stories in Hebrew. The first of these, "Shem Veyefet Ba'agala" ("Shem and Japhet in the Train Compartment") appeared in 1890. This is a rather curious little story in which Mendele describes his first trip in, of all things, a train. The story opens as Mendele describes the differences between the Jews, who push and shove each other in the crowded third class section, and the gentiles, who wait calmly until the train is ready to leave before they go to their reserved seats in the other sections. There is, in this description, a complete sense of separation: the two groups have no contact at all. Inside the compartment, Mendele is quite uncomfortable with his traveling companions, a large family of poor Jews from Germany. He feels trapped and he misses the freedom of his wagon; but soon, when a non-Jew appears and acts like part of the family, Mendele's curiosity is aroused and he joins in conversation with them. From Moshe, the father, Mendele learns that he and the non-Jew, whom they call Japhet instead of trying to pronounce his real name, Przecsczwinczicki, were at one time close friends, even venturing to discuss their religious differences in an amiable way. Eventually, however, Japhet fell under the sway of anti-Semites and turned on his former friend. After the eastern Jews were expelled from Prussia, Moshe and his family wandered through the Pale, and one day Moshe helped rescue Japhet, who had been expelled from Prussia for being a Pole. Moshe educated Japhet in the ways of living in exile, of being a wanderer, and Japhet has been a part of the wandering family ever since.

Near the beginning of the story, Abramovitsh clearly lets us know that the events in the story took place in 1880, just before the pogroms, so that the story is full of dramatic irony. Thus, as Mendele leaves the train and sees Japhet making arrangements with the conductor for the comfort of the family, he says, "Lord of the universe! Grant us but a few more such disciples—and Shem and Japhet will be brothers—and peace will come to Israel"[12] We know, of course, that in its context this hope was futile, that Shem and Japhet, the two sons of Noah who had cooperated in concealing their father's shame and who had sired the Semitic and Aryan races, respectively, were destined to remain apart. The Germans, Moshe tells Mendele, have brought back the time of the Flood, the time of chaos and human depravity, and have made Shem and Japhet into enemies; but as Moshe shows, and as we saw earlier in "Beseter Ra'am," Shem and Japhet depend on each other and must learn to get along or both will be ruined. In 1880, this might have seemed meaningful, but by 1890 such hopes had to be tempered by the knowledge of the pogroms, by the knowledge that Japhet had once again rejected Shem. Much more important is the description Moshe gives Pan Przecsczwinszicki of how the Jews have survived by sticking together, even to the extent of having rich people treat the poor like members of their own families.

Of course Moshe's praise of the Jews belies a great deal of Abramovitsh's other writings, but in the late years of the nineteenth century he was often more interested in promoting Jewish solidarity than in describing Jewish divisiveness. Such divisiveness, however, is the theme of Abramovitsh's next story, "Lo Nachat be'Ya'akov" ("There Is no Good in Jacob"). The Yiddish title of the story is "Di Alte Mayse" ("The Old Story"), and it is, in fact, the same old story we have heard time and again, for, as Mendele points out in the brief prologue to the Yiddish version, the book of Ecclesiastes says that there is nothing new under the sun. The story concerns two men, Benjamin, an old, scholarly, religious, and soft-spoken man, and Reb Ya'akov, a power-mongering hypocrite in the style of

Yitzchok-Avrom. Everyone in their small town depends on Benjamin for his advice, even the non-Jews who drink in his wife's inn. Reb Ya'akov, on the other hand, whose rise to power is described in terms of a butterfly's development, beginning as a worm, is respected only by those people whose financial destiny he controls, though he constantly tries to force his way into intellectual conversations, only to have his own ignorance thrown in his face. Nevertheless, "when Jews see a pile of money near someone, whoever he may be, even if he is a calf, an animal in the form of a man, they raise him to the level of a god, they bow to him, they dance before him, they flatter him, they honor his name" (371).[13] His companions praise him throughout the town and call him "Rabbi Ya'akov," and everyone responds in awe, "Blessed be his name." Only a few people in town refuse to believe in Reb Ya'akov, but, Mendele tells us ironically, for allowing these heretics to remain, the town is punished with a plague of controversies. In the meantime, Reb Ya'akov assumes control over various religious duties, over ritual slaughtering, over the meat tax, over running the hospital, and over the yeshiva, though only his wife thinks of him as a scholar. The only person who shows no fear of him is Benjamin, and naturally the hypocrite resents the old man. His resentment becomes even stronger when a terrible famine hits the region and there is a town meeting to decide what the people should do: should they stay and pray, should they move to another district in the Pale, or should they join the movement to found Jewish colonies in Africa. All along there has been a great deal of Talmudic discussion on the matter, but as Mendele says, "The Talmud was magnified not for the sake of practical judgments, but for the sake of pilpul, of being able to show off in complex discussions" (373). Reb Ya'akov says they should remain in town, largely because he has just raised the meat tax in order to support his relatives. Benjamin, however, explains that all of Jewish history, even from the time of Abraham, has been expressed in the words that God addressed to the first patriarch: "Go forth." Like Moshe in "Shem and Japhet," Benjamin sees Jewish existence as a series of removes from one place to another, and he therefore counsels the people to go elsewhere, wherever they want, " 'for you all have one Father and you are one nation, the children of Israel. Go, my brothers, and the Lord God will have pity on you and bless you' " (375). Reb Ya'akov, however, announces that Benjamin's advice is a profanation, since it shows no faith that God will save the people. When everyone ignores him, he resolves to avenge himself on Benjamin.

Another cause for Reb Ya'akov's hatred arises when the Haskala strikes the town, again like a plague. Suddenly the son-in-law of one of Ya'akov's followers is caught with a modern book, and Ya'akov becomes a fanatical persecutor of Maskilim, largely because he fears that the Haskala will cost him business. Benjamin, on the other hand, in a very moving and highly unrealistic scene, holds a long conversation with the Maskilim, in which he points out the dangers of secular learning. The Jew, he says, is like a tree in winter: it appears to be dead, but within it flows the sap that will give it life in the spring. The life-giving substance in the Jew is his religion and as long as the Maskilim preserve their Judaism, they are free to study anything they want. "Benjamin's words, which came from his heart, entered the hearts of the young men. With tears on their cheeks they grasped his hand and swore that they would remember his words forever" (377). All this, of course, is reminiscent of *Dos Vintshfingerl* and indicates again how Abramovitsh was struggling with the problem of the Haskala.

The story ends as Reb Ya'akov uses his wealth and his political connections to drive Benjamin's wife out of business and eventually to her death. Although everyone in town recognizes the injustice, no one will speak out to oppose Reb Ya'akov. "The people of our village, like flawless sacrificial sheep, kept silent and trembled, grew poorer and didn't open their mouths" (378). The most that anyone does is to whisper a curse against Ya'akov into Mendele's ear, and Mendele, seeing how everyone pretends not to be concerned in the matter, only laughs a tearful laugh.

Obviously this is the same story we have heard over and over again from Abramovitsh. It tells of corruption among the rich, weakness and passivity among the oppressed; it tells of disaster for the good man and dissension among the Jews. But Abramovitsh was not simply repeating himself for want of a new topic. Rather, he was emphasizing that there was nothing basically new in the current situation (an idea underscored by the mention of Korach, the biblical type of the man who pretended to act for the good of all, but who was actually motivated by personal desire) and that the old solutions, if properly applied, would still work. Thus "Lo Nachat be'Ya'akov" reaffirms the validity of the early Haskala approach to the problems. And yet, as Benjamin says in his discourse on "Go

forth," and as Abramovitsh says in his Yiddish title, there is no end
in sight, no sign of respite for the Jews anywhere, especially as long
as factionalism based on selfish interests continues to exist.

Abramovitsh's next story shows Mendele trying—and
rejecting—a new solution. The story, "Bymey Hara'ash" ("In the
Days of Tumult"), published in 1894, describes a curious incident in
Mendele's life. After the pogroms he lost his taste for being a book
peddler, partly because he thought that books were worthless in the
face of Jewish problems. So with a band of Kabtsansk Jews he decided to emigrate to Palestine. Most of the story is set in Odessa,
where Mendele has come with his friend Lieb the Teacher. Immediately we recognize that this work fits in with Abramovitsh's late
stories, as Mendele expresses disappointment over their poor reception by the Odessa Jewish community. Primarily the story contrasts Lieb's tragicomic blind trust in the promises of Zionism
(reminiscent of the dreams of the Tuneyadevka Jews in *Benjamin
the Third*) with Mendele's growing skepticism. At one point Mendele even tries to convince himself that Lieb's blind trust is superior
to knowledge—that, in effect, ignorance is bliss—and he vows to
have more faith; but his evil spirit destroys this faith rather easily:
" 'You need bread and you trust in faith' " (413), he says, and Mendele quickly realizes that he cannot be like the simple souls of
Tuneyadevka. In fact Mendele feels himself divided in two: one
Mendele is trusting and gullible and really wants to believe that
emigrating will solve his problems while the other Mendele is cynical and realistic. Finally Mendele is called to the house of one of the
city's leading Zionists and the two men have an important
meeting—both for Mendele and for our understanding of Abramovitsh's position on this crucial issue.

The Zionist explains to Mendele that the Zionist ideology states
that the Jews' problems will be ended when they have a homeland
of their own. The Zionists' original plans called for gradual coloniza-
tion by young people who would be able to handle the hard physical
labor of carving a livable place out of the deserts and swamps of
Palestine. However, he says, the idea of the colonies so caught
everyone's imagination that the Zionists have been inundated by
crowds of potential emigrants who could not possibly handle the
work; and furthermore, the Zionists are not receiving the kind of
financial support they need because the Jews are too disorganized.
This last comment leads Mendele to a long defense of Jewish dis-

unity: if the Jews were all united, he explains, they would be more easily destroyed. It is their divisiveness that has preserved them. " 'Every Jew is a small nation unto himself. When you oppress one, the other feels nothing . . .' " (416). This does not describe lack of feeling among the Jews (though it could be seen that way if Mendele is to be regarded ironically), but rather the historical reality that, because of their dispersion, the Jews have never been attacked as a whole.

The Zionist is impressed by Mendele's words, but he says that they ignore the present problem. Right now the Jews need young laborers for Palestine and writers to combat the charlatans who control Jewish life. In a passage that recalls *Di Klyatshe* and paraphrases Psalm 114, the Zionist tells how to deal with the charlatans, the Yitzchok-Avroms and their kind: " 'Pour ink upon them. . . . Before the drop of ink even Satan flees, and before the power of books even Asmodeus will turn back' " (417). Mendele can best help the Jews by staying, by continuing to sell his books and spread enlightenment. His books are not, as he thought, worthless; and the salvation of the Jews is a community effort in which everyone must play his part, in which factionalism and self-aggrandizement are out of place.

Recognizing the truth in these words, Mendele returns to Kabtsansk, Lieb having found a position as a teacher in Odessa. Back in Glupsk, where he feels like a frog back in water, Mendele buys a load of books and rescues his poor horse from the cruel man to whom he had sold it. Again, without making too close an identification between Mendele and Abramovitsh, a parallel is clear. Mendele has to return to Glupsk to rescue his nag and to be of service to the Jews. Abramovitsh has to defend his work as a writer: he cannot simply pick up and go to Palestine, leaving the mass of people behind. Zionism has its good points, but is not a panacea and he, as a writer, must stay behind, must continue pouring his ink on the enemies of Israel. Like a clear-sighted Isrulik, he must rescue and defend his nag. He is not one of Asmodeus' servants, one of the Maskilim who condescended to and oppressed the common people; he is one of their saviors, and he must stay in Glupsk and continue his important work. Like *Dos Vintshfingerl*, "Bymey Hara'ash" is, among other things, a work of self-defense.

One other major story deals with similar themes, "Byshiva shel Ma'alah Uvyshiva shel Mata" ("In the Heavenly and Earthly Assemblies"), published in 1894–1895. This story, a bit too long and rambling, describes Mendele's stay in Warsaw during a pogrom. The "heavenly assembly" is what he calls the group of Jews who were hiding with him in an attic during the pogrom. This group consists of Eliahu, a Lithuanian Jew (Lithuanians were noted for their skepticism and their opposition to Hasidism); Reb Shimshon, a wealthy Hasid; Albert, a modern, assimilated Jew; and Shmuel and Ya'akov, two rather simple Jews. Obviously this group represents the various factions that opposed each other in late nineteenth century Judaism; but because of the crisis, the five men, along with Mendele, gradually coalesce into a unified group, with even Albert proclaiming himself to be a Jew and asking to be called by his Hebrew name.

The "earthly assembly" consists of the group of men whom Mendele encounters at his inn after he leaves the attic. In this group are Reb Israel, a Lithuanian Jew; and Benzion, Segol, and Katz, three Zionists. Here again we have many pages of discussion over the merits of various positions, and Mendele, throughout, is in a kind of agony, since all of the speakers seem right to him: he agrees with Reb Israel that the Jews should trust in God, but he also agrees with the Zionists, especially when one of them begins to praise the Haskala for having given birth to their movement and for having tried to raise the quality of life. Once more Mendele defends the dispersion of the Jews as God's way of preserving them, but the Zionists accuse him of inaction, describing him in terms similar to those he used to describe the Jews of Tuneyadevka in *Benjamin the Third*: they say that while he waits for the Messiah to come, they are ready to take action. The discussion ends, of course, with nothing settled, but what we see is that no one faction has the answer to the Jewish problem, and in fact, in spite of Mendele's assertions, the extreme diversity of the Jews, along with their inability to compromise, really brings harm. All of the factions present a part of the truth; but as long as they remain factions, the whole truth will never come together. One of the most important passages in the story is the Zionist's praise of the Haskala, for his speech represents a kind of understanding of and a possible solution to the harmful factionalism that besets the Jews.

When Mendele finds that he has lost his money, however, he goes to both Albert and Shimshon, and both of them refuse to acknowledge him. Now that the crisis has passed, they have returned to their factionalism and Mendele can only get home because another simple merchant lets him have books on credit. Similarly, on the train home, Albert and Shimshon acknowledge Mendele when they are in trouble, but Shmuel and Ya'akov recognize him at once and are happy to see him. The Korahs, those who comprise the various factions only for their own benefit, keep the Jews divided, but the simple merchants and the common Jews, whatever their faults, demonstrate a kind of unity.

These late works—*Dos Vintshfingerl* and the short stories—show Abramovitsh struggling, after the 1881 pogroms and in the face of new oppression, to strengthen the Jewish people by bringing them closer together, by trying to overcome their factionalism. Part of this effort involved a defense of his own life's work and a reaffirmation of the Haskala. His works still contain a great emphasis on the needs of this world as opposed to the hopes for the other world; but the first person narrative in the short stories also allows us to see Mendele's dealings with the problems, his uncertainty. The relatively clear answers of *Dos Kleyne Mentshele* and *Di Takse* are too simple. Mendele—and it is not pushing too much occasionally to see Abramovitsh reflected in Mendele—must struggle with the new complexities of the Jewish problems. That the struggle is not resolved in Abramovitsh's fiction is not surprising when we consider that many of the same problems remain in our time.

CHAPTER 8

Shloyme Reb Khayims:
A Time to Keep

I *Mendele and Abramovitsh*

A BRAMOVITSH'S last years were spent primarily in revising his works and enjoying his reputation as the *Zayda*, the Grandfather of Yiddish literature. This title had been bestowed on him by Sholem Aleichem, who was trying to establish a tradition for Yiddish literature; and the aging writer, freed to an extent from his earlier financial worries, enjoyed the role. After the pogroms of 1905, Abramovitsh left Russia and spent two years in Geneva (the setting for Sholem Aleichem's essay "Fir Zenen Mir Gezesn," in which Abramovitsh is pictured as an archetypal grandfather), but he then returned to Russia where, in 1909, he made a triumphal tour of Jewish cities. His last few years he spent ill and partially paralyzed, dying on December 8, 1917, at the age of eighty-one. Despite fame and illness, his mind continued to dwell on the problems he had raised and examined throughout his life, and they appear again in his last important work, the incomplete autobiographical novel *Shloyme Reb Khayims* (*Shloyme, the Son of Reb Khayim*; in Hebrew *Bayamim Hahem* [*Of Bygone Days*]) which appeared, as we now have it, in 1911.

Shloyme Reb Khayims is a fascinating work for a number of reasons, not least of which is that it presents the first face-to-face confrontation between Abramovitsh, who is the titular hero, and Mendele, who visits him in Odessa. Forty-seven years after his first appearance in *Dos Kleyne Mentshele*, Mendele, having aged not at all, tells in the preface about his arrival in Odessa and he begins, like Fishke, to complain about the city, which is not at all to his taste. After an allegorical description of the recent weather, in reality a description of recent Jewish history with its promise of spring obliterated by winter storms, Mendele heads for the home of Shloyme,

152

whom he claims to have known for a long time. He supports this
claim by telling some of Shloyme's history, including his work about
Glupsk (Berdichev) and his decision to leave Glupsk and concentrate on another group of people, probably the Maskilim, though
this phase did not last long either: "Perhaps he got tired of them too,
perhaps he decided that he would rather make his living by skinning
carcasses than by dealing with creatures of their kind" (258).[1] Mendele, of course, is ironic here, since the satirist's job has traditionally
been described in terms of flaying, of skinning away the externals in
order to expose the hypocrisy beneath. Thus Shloyme's new course
was not new at all: Abramovitsh insists on his role as a satirist
throughout his career, though aside from the preface this is his least
satiric work.

When Mendele finally arrives at Shloyme's house, he finds the
old author discussing literature with three Hebrew writers. Naturally Mendele joins the discussion, telling the authors that "writing
is lunacy, a kind of weakness and folly of the ego, like the compul-
sion of some people to step to the pulpit and treat the congregation
to a sampling of their gargling" (261). Shloyme responds with a
high-flown speech about reason and the finest use of language, but
the others rightly object that he is talking about the kind of flowery
but empty language that to their minds characterizes modern literature, in which authors merely harangue, and in which each author,
as one of them says, " 'is the Adam of his age, inventing the alphabet
all over again' " (262). Thus, by seeming to praise modern literature,
Abramovitsh actually damns it, showing the weakness of its theory.

As Shloyme begins to clarify his approach to literature, there is a
sudden commotion, when a young student comes seeking shelter for
the night. Shloyme rudely throws the boy out into the storm (with
all its allegorical implications) and returns to his friends, but they
are all so affected by the interruption that the party soon breaks up.
The next evening, when they are all together again, Shloyme explains that he has a new perception of what they had been talking
about, for the poor student reminded him of himself, and he sincerely repents his rudeness. The impoverished young man has
made the sophisticated and successful old writer aware of his own
past and the relationship between that past and his present situation. As his friends urge him to write his memoirs, to preserve his
people's life in literature, Shloyme continues to think back to his
early years, his discovery of the joy of life and of nature's splendor;

and he suddenly returns to the previous day's discussion. He is, he explains, torn between the present, which he often feels is worthless when compared to the past, and the past, which he realizes is dead and hardly worth dwelling on. This, of course, is part of the problem we saw in Abramovitsh's approach to *Dos Vintshfingerl*, where he tried to describe and defend the past without really defining his relationship to it. Consequently the novel ended in confusion. Now, recognizing that the world of *Ha'avot Vehabanim*, of *Dos Kleyne Mentshele*, of his own childhood, has largely disappeared, he is drawn to it again, prodded by the appearance of the poor student. " 'My mind is now completely in the world of my youth. I have returned to it an old, bitter man, worn by hard experience, my heart wounded by the arrows of life's battles' " (271).

Still, he is reluctant to write about that time, which he describes to his friends—including Mendele, who, in effect, still lives in what is left of that time—as " 'ugly, devoid of pleasure and satisfaction, with not a single ray of light to pierce the continual darkness . . .' " (272). There is nothing in such a life that would interest modern readers, he says. Strangely, Mendele and the modern Hebrew writers object to Shloyme's words, arguing that the bitterness is an important part of Jewish life. Furthermore, they say, " 'Even though the life of the Jewish people seems repulsive from the outside, it is pleasant enough within. . . . The thunder and lightning that occasionally overtake the Jews purge them and renew their vigor . . . Under a pile of dirt in the *cheder* and the yeshiva and study-house the fire of Torah blazes, radiating light and warmth to our people. . . . It is altogether fitting and proper that such a life be set down in a permanent record' " (273). This theme, the inner beauty of an externally ugly life, has appeared in Abramovitsh's works in varying degrees since *Ha'avot Vehabanim*. Once again we are reminded that inside the nag lives a prince, that it is their religion that has sustained the Jews. But now we go a step further, for the modern big city writers and the old *shtetl* Mendele all agree that Jewish life—the old, traditional Jewish life—is a worthwhile subject for literature, even if, as Shloyme says, it lacks the ingredients that modern readers seek.

Once again Shloyme seeks to dissuade his friends, this time by arguing that even if they are correct about the old Jewish life, there is nothing special about him to make his life worth recording. Here, in his argument that " 'We are an ant-hill, in which the individual has no existence apart from the community' " (274), he sounds like Ahad Ha'am, whose nationalistic theories, in reality, did not please Abramovitsh. Naturally Shloyme's friends object again, pointing out that every individual is different and that it is his duty—his duty to the past, to traditional Jewish life, as well as to the present—to write an autobiography.

Shloyme's final objection, that he cannot go through the trouble of having the book published, is dismissed by Mendele, who volunteers to do the work. Shloyme, then, agrees to write his autobiography, and the preface ends. The importance of this preface is that it shows Abramovitsh having worked out many of the problems that crippled *Dos Vintshfingerl*. In fact, though *Shloyme Reb Khayims* ends when Shloyme is thirteen, at the death of his father, it seems to follow the same course that Abramovitsh had outlined for *Dos Vintshfingerl*. It shows every indication of becoming a detailed, panoramic picture of Eastern European Jewish life in the nineteenth century, developed by focusing on Shloyme's life. This time, however, thanks to the long preface, there is no need for propaganda and self-defense. The preface presents and explains the problem and reaffirms the possibility—the necessity—for Jewish literature, literature about Jewish themes, as well as for Yiddish literature, literature on all subjects, written in Yiddish. Implicit here is the understanding that a national literature involves more than simply a common language: it requires a knowledge of the nation and of the individuals who comprise it. Abramovitsh, of course, knew this from the beginning of his career, but as Yiddish literature developed, thanks largely to his efforts, writers began to forget this important point.

Abramovitsh again demonstrated his brilliance—and humor—in constructing this preface. It was funny when Fishke saw Abramovitsh in Odessa and expressed his disbelief that this man could be a Jewish teacher; but now Mendele, the intermediary in *Fishke*, must prompt Abramovitsh to tell his story, just as he had been forced to prod Fishke. This is especially interesting because the story itself, autobiographical as it is, must bridge the gulf between the old world of Abramovitsh's youth and the new world of his old age. Thus Mendele, who might be expected to share Fishke's attitude toward the "Frenchified" modern, actually encourages his old friend to move ahead by combining the old traditional world with the new, to preserve the old world by treating it in a new way,

through literature. The spectacle of Mendele, in his traditional
garb, joining company with the three modern writers to encourage
Abramovitsh, is both ironic and funny. But it is also quite serious,
for Mendele has gradually realized in the later stories—in his train
trips, in his stays in large cities—that the world has changed. In
spite of his disparaging comments on Odessa at the beginning of the
preface, he knows that even Glupsk is no longer a *shtetl*. It is, as we
saw in *Dos Vintshfingerl*, a big city filled with corruption. The
shtetl, perhaps in spite of itself, has been brought into the modern
world, and Abramovitsh has the duty to preserve it and reconcile it
to its new conditions. In an important sense, here, at the end of his
career, Abramovitsh has returned to his starting point in *Ha'avot
Vehabanim*, where he tried to bring the people to Haskala, to the
modern world, to show that the movement to Haskala was an accomplished fact. Now, more than forty years later, having increased
in compassion, having taken the people's side, he is trying much the
same thing, with the important difference that the Haskala, in spite
of its failings and in concert with a number of other movements, has
begun to triumph over the old life.

Shloyme Reb Khayims, then, according to the preface, should be
an enormously long work of the greatest importance. Unfortunately,
Abramovitsh had completed relatively little of it by 1911. (In later
chapters, his conception of the work seems to have changed, so that
it is probably best to consider only the first part here.) What we
have in the autobiography itself is a long description of Kapulie, and
the story of Shloyme's life until the death of his father. (The opening
chapter shows the family's plight after the father's death, and Abramovitsh obviously intended to begin the story *in medias res*, emphasizing its epic nature. Because of the book's abrupt ending, this
structural device is less effective than it might have been.) There is
little here in the way of plot: Shloyme is born into a religious and
fairly wealthy family; he receives a typical Jewish education with
some modern learning thrown in; he is a prodigy but is tempted
away from his studies by his love of nature; and suddenly his father
dies and his family is plunged into poverty. The story, aside from
whatever autobiographical details we can pick up, is of secondary
importance in this work. Much more important are the descriptions
of life in Kapulie: the role of women, the life of children, the relationship of the people to nature, and the status of craftsmen.

One of the most touching scenes in the book describes, for exam-

ple, the prayer recited by Shloyme's mother as she makes candles
for the Day of Atonement, asking for purification from sin, for protection for Jewish children (this was at the time when children were
kidnapped for the czar's army), for good teachers, and for protection
against anti-Semitism. This is a simple prayer, but Abramovitsh
adds

If anyone can find it in his heart to laugh at this prayer, or mock it, let him
do so. But then let *him* point to souls as pure as these. Let *him* duplicate
these tender feelings, these burning tears, this love of Torah and wisdom,
this regard for one's fellow man and all mankind.

Better yet, let him listen carefully to the prayers of these Jewish women,
and discover what the "Jewish heart" is all about. Let him listen . . . and
hold his peace forever. (302)

This passage illustrates the theme of the preface, for here Abramovitsh, devoting himself to a strictly Jewish scene, describes the old
and asserts its continuing vitality and relevance. The simple prayer,
expressing both the horrors of Jewish existence in the Pale and the
redeeming faith in God's benevolent protection, confirms the words
of the preface, that Jewish life is externally ugly but internally beautiful.

Some of life's beauty, however, is denied the Jews, especially the
children. Throughout his novels, Abramovitsh bemoans the life of
Jewish children, who are exposed so early to life's hardships that
they seem to pass directly from infancy to adulthood, skipping
childhood completely. In the autobiography he refers to the "Jewish
child, who is expected to act like a full-fledged Jew before he has
learned to walk, whose childhood flits by like a dream, leaving him a
gloomy old man before his time" (330). This situation was the result
not only of external pressures and economic hardship (as it is in the
world Dickens describes), but of the Jewish method of education,
another of Abramovitsh's favorite themes. Although Jews venerated
the Torah, they regarded some parts as more worthy of study than
others. Thus, when a young boy began going to school, he first
studied not the interesting Bible stories but the much duller law
codes of Leviticus. In fact, we are told, "Fathers kept their sons
from studying the Bible as from something that smacked of
freethinking" (294). Secular subjects were almost never studied,
though Shloyme's father taught them, as well as the whole Bible, to

his son. Nevertheless, "in the present world, Shloymele was a dunce, utterly ignorant of life, but in the world of his studies he was brilliant and well informed. . . . Perfectly at home in the past . . . he found there a perfect whirl of activities. . . . Shloymele was quite busy in the world of the past, where his real life was lived" (311). All his fantasies, all his knowledge of the world were inspired by biblical and Talmudic texts. He took no joy from the present, but dwelt in the world of two thousand years ago. In a statement that covers a number of aspects of the problem, we are told that "to exist in memory of the past, to stand in the middle of history, circling back to the same spot again and again, refusing to budge forward an inch—this is not living, but dreaming" (304). Although religious traditions are important, and have preserved the Jewish people, they should not be allowed to become self-consuming. This, unfortunately, is what happened in the Pale. For Shloyme, this world was "only a passageway to the next; what difference should it make to a Jew, even a grown-up Jew with a beard, if the passageway was a bit cramped and not very pretty"? (319).

Soon, however, Shloyme became aware of the real world, and especially of natural beauty. Suddenly he began to neglect his studies in order to wander through the fields. Of course such an attachment to nature was foreign to Judaism at the time, and Shloyme's new obsession was regarded by his elders—and by himself—as the work of an evil spirit, an idea that also runs through Abramovitsh's short story "The Calf," written at about the same time as the autobiography. In fact, one of Abramovitsh's important innovations in Yiddish and Hebrew literature was his devotion to and use of nature. Not only was he aware of it, already something new in Yiddish literature, but he employed it as a structural device as early as 1862 in *Limdu Hetev*. Clearly his devotion to nature began in his youth and was an important force in carrying him from the ancient world to the modern.

Not only was the young Shloyme attracted by nature, but he also fell briefly under the influence of something even worse—love. As we saw in *Ha'avot Vehabanim*, romantic love was not a part of Jewish existence. So distant was it from the Jewish experience that it hardly appears even in Abramovitsh's work from *Dos Kleyne Mentshele* until *Dos Vintshfingerl*, and Abramovitsh advised Sholem Aleichem not to write about it. Even in *Dos Vintshfingerl* it was handled rather clumsily. In *Shloyme Reb Khayims*, it plays a very small part, but Abramovitsh's comment on Shloyme's love is interesting: "Even had it been possible to see into his heart, no one would have had the least understanding of his thoughts. Love is not the kind of thing the Jewish mind can grasp" (324). Immediately, however, he follows this harsh criticism with a warm and loving description of Jewish family life, which contains the seeds of love that have not been allowed to blossom. Shloyme's romance was brief and uneventful, but it set him off from the people around him.

Finally, "the last stage in his voyage out of the world of the past" (337) was marked by his attachment to Isaac the blacksmith and Hertzl the carpenter, two craftsmen who, more than anyone else the boy had ever known, had managed to preserve a kind of simple, childish joy for life. They were not trapped in the life of two thousand years ago and therefore did not have to put constraints on their enjoyment of life. But again, Shloyme's affection for them set him off from other respectable people: not only did Isaac and Hertzl partake of life, but they were only craftsmen, and we know from *Dos Kleyne Mentshele* how craftsmen were regarded. In fact, Abramovitsh could not keep himself from describing once more, at the end of his career, the scorn with which people looked down on craftsmen and the wretched system by which they were trained.

It should be obvious that *Shloyme Reb Khayims* offers relatively little new in Abramovitsh's thought, though many of the old themes are well handled. In an important sense, this last work is Abramovitsh's recapitulation, overview, and assessment of his own career. The mere fact that he must try to reconcile the old and the new indicates how much change had taken place, often in the direction he had favored. When he says that "by their own standards the Jewish craftsmen were a lowly group in those days" (334), the last phrase tells us that progress has been made. In many respects, Jewish life is still an *alte mayse*, an old story, but there is change. Unlike *Dos Vintshfingerl*, which gave us propaganda in defense of the old values, *Shloyme Reb Khayims* offers living examples of the old values and illustrates their worth in the modern world—so long as they do not become stultified, hollow forms. And though this last work may gloss over some of the problems that we know existed, its sense of progress, spirituality, and preserved tradition makes it a fitting work with which to end our study of Abramovitsh.

II *Conclusion*

It is difficult to offer any final assessment of Abramovitsh's work and its influence on subsequent authors. If we can keep our sense of proportion, we might compare him to Chaucer, for both writers discovered the literary powers of their respective languages and brought forth impressive bodies of work. Indeed, had it not been for Hitler and Stalin, Yiddish literature would still be flourishing; but the Holocaust did not put an end to Abramovitsh's influence, for he affected generations of Yiddish writers who affected generations of American writers. Not only are Yiddish authors like Sholem Aleichem and Peretz his heirs, but so, whether they have read him or not, are such authors as Saul Bellow, Bernard Malamud, Joseph Heller, and Philip Roth. Even a travesty like *Portnoy's Complaint*, with its pretense of satiric self-criticism, has its roots in Abramovitsh.

In addition to his strictly literary influence, Abramovitsh also had an important linguistic influence. His later Hebrew stories were significant in the development of modern Hebrew, and his strict attention to Yiddish style and language gave impetus to the standardization of written Yiddish and the important work in this area undertaken by the YIVO Institute. Largely through his efforts, Yiddish attained a status that in the early nineteenth century would have been unthinkable. Prior to Abramovitsh no one could have conceived that before the century was over a Harvard professor, Leo Wiener, would write a book called *Yiddish Literature in the Nineteenth Century*. How could anyone write literature in jargon, in a language that was not really a language? Abramovitsh showed that it could be done by showing that Yiddish was, in fact, a highly developed language, with a dignity all its own. As he recognized early in his career, Yiddish was not simply corrupt German. It was the authentic expression of the Jewish masses. His insistence that he labored over every word and phrase and his refusal to allow editors—even Sholem Aleichem—to change his spelling (which in his time was not standardized) offers further proof of his respect for Yiddish. One result of his glorification of the language was to raise the status of the Jewish masses in their own eyes and in the eyes of many Maskilim. Certainly he was arrogant when he refused to consider himself in the same class as other Yiddish writers; but he was also justified, for he transformed Yiddish literature from propaganda into art. Once he had cleared the path, other writers no longer needed to prove that Yiddish was worthy of literary consideration, so that the other giants of Yiddish literature, from Sholem Aleichem and Peretz through the brothers Singer, could approach their work in a different spirit.

One other area in which Abramovitsh is most important, though there is some controversy about this point, is as a historian. He told his friend Shimon Dubnov that anyone who wanted to know about life in the Pale would have to consult his works, and, as Joshua Rothenberg says, "it became a kind of cliché that if you wanted to know the life of the Jews of that period, you had to read Mendele."[2] While Rothenberg presents a cogent argument against Mendele's value as an historian, Mark Zborowski and Elizabeth Herzog list him as one of their major sources in their study of the *shtetl*.[3] Other critics are equally divided over this problem. It would perhaps be more accurate to say that Abramovitsh was a historian of the *shtetl*, in which most of his works are set, and that his description of Jewish life in the cities is not as fully developed. Although much of his work consists of caricature, there is an unmistakable feeling of realism in the novels. As with Dickens, though much of his work is caricature and satire, we leave his world with a real sense of having been there, a sense that now we really know what that world was like.

Abramovitsh is often described only as a satirist, as a writer who described and exposed the sterility of life in the Pale. This assessment is correct, as far as it goes; but it only describes one aspect of his work, for he did not confine himself to satire and he saw more than sterility in the life around him. He was outraged at the corruption of community leaders, at the passivity of the masses, at the inhumanity exhibited by anti-Semitic governments, and at the generally horrible life the people were forced to live. In his outrage he resembles Swift, one of his favorite authors. But he also understood some of the problems of the community leaders, he tried to analyze the people's passivity, he tried to encourage good relations between the Jews and the governments, he tried to give dignity to the people. To say that his works only depict the sterility of life in the Pale is to misrepresent. His works deal with sterility because he is analyzing it, often indicating that the sterility is only superficial, that beneath the outer appearance lies a vibrancy, a vitality informed by spirituality, that enables Jews to suffer and to endure, to see brightness where others see only misery, and to triumph over the difficulty of their lives. This aspect became especially important after *Di Klyatshe,* and it continued even after the pogroms in works like *Fishke der Krumer.* Sterility is not the major focus of Abramovitsh's work. Perhaps because of his background in the Haskala, as well as because of his own innate compassion, he is more often positive than negative. He did not simply attack the people, telling them that their lives were sterile. Rather, he stood with them and encouraged them to persevere by giving them a sense of their own worth. Certainly he was critical, but his criticism, like that of a good parent, was full of love.

Abramovitsh, throughout his life, was concerned with the day-to-day life of his people, not with the metaphysical problems behind that life or with the dark recesses of man's soul. Occasionally Mendele will question God's ways, even to the point of blasphemy, or another character will ask why the Jews must suffer, but the closest we ever get to an answer is Mendele's "Ta, ta, ta." Abramovitsh recognized the metaphysical questions, but he concentrated on the world around him. Like the author of Ecclesiastes, he knew that God is there, but he also knew that people cannot wait for miracles, that they must understand their situation and take action to better that situation. This theme runs through the entire progression of his works. For all these reasons, those works were vitally important to Jews—and non-Jews—in the nineteenth century, and they remain important today.

Notes and References

Preface

1. Charles A. Madison, *Yiddish Literature: Its Scope and Major Writers* (New York: Frederick Ungar, 1968), p. 60.

Chapter One

1. Isaac Bashevis Singer, *Enemies: A Love Story* (New York: Farrar, Straus & Giroux, 1972), p. 163.
2. This work has been translated by Dan Ben-Amos and Jerome R. Mintz as *In Praise of the Baal Shem Tov* (Bloomington: Indiana University Press, 1970).
3. *King Artus: A Hebrew Arthurian Romance of 1279*, ed. and trans. Curt Leviant (New York: Ktav Publishing House, 1969).
4. Translated as *The Shepherd Prince: A Historical Romance of the Days of Isaiah*, trans. Benjamin Schapiro (New York: Brookside Publishing Co., 1922).
5. For fuller accounts of various aspects of this period, see the Selected Bibliography, Section II.

Chapter Two

1. Dan Miron, ed., Introduction, *Learn to Do Well* (New York: YIVO Institute for Jewish Research, 1969), p. vi.
2. *Ibid.*, p. vi.
3. All references are to *Ha'avot Vehabanim* in *Kol Kitvey Mendele Mocher Seforim* (Tel Aviv: Hotsa'at Dvir, 1947). All translations are my own.
4. Miron, p. 22.
5. *Ibid.*, Fourth Supplement, pp. 116–25.
6. *Ibid.*, pp. 28ff.

Chapter Three

1. Abramovitsh, *Eyn Mishpat*, quoted in M. Viner, *Tsu der Geshikhte fun der Yidisher Literatur in 19-tn Yorhundert*, vol. 2 (New York: Yiddisher Kultur Farband, 1946), p. 15. My translation.

2. Gerald Stillman's English translation is called *The Parasite* (New York: Thomas Yoseloff, 1956). Unless otherwise noted, all quotations are from this translation.

3. I must refer the reader to Dan Miron, *A Traveler Disguised* (New York: Schocken Books, 1973) for a detailed discussion of Mendele's role in Abramovitsh's fiction.

4. This is, by and large, the version presented in Stillman's translation.

5. The Talmud Torah was the community-supported school whose purpose was to educate boys whose families could not afford to send them to better schools.

6. Ronald Paulson, *Satire and the Novel in Eighteenth-Century England* (New Haven: Yale University Press, 1967), p. 25.

7. Sholem Aleichem, "Fir Zenen Mir Gezesn," in *Ale Verk fun Mendele Mocher Seforim*, ed. N. Maysl (Warsaw: Farlag Mendele, 1928), vol. 21, p. 33. My translation.

8. Ronald Paulson, *The Fictions of Satire* (Baltimore: Johns Hopkins University Press, 1967), p. 59.

9. *Ale Verk* (1928), 2, 57.

10. *Ibid.*, p. 140.

11. *Ibid.*, p. 45.

12. *Ibid.*, p. 133.

13. *Service for the Day of Atonement*, with an English translation by S. G. (New York: Hebrew Publishing Company, 1928), p. 154.

14. *Ale Verk*, (1928), 2, 133–37. My translation.

15. This view of the Talmud Torah and the *rebbeh* can be found in many works of Jewish literature. In *The Russian Jew under Tsars and Soviets* (New York: Macmillan, 1964), Salo W. Baron defends the institution and its teachers.

16. *Ale Verk* (1928), 2, 142. My translation.

17. *Ibid.*, p. 79.

18. For other works that deal with problems concerning women's role in Eastern European Judaism, see Isaac Joel Linetzki's *The Polish Lad*, trans. Moshe Spiegel (Philadelphia: Jewish Publication Society of America, 1975), and Chaim Grade's *The Agunah*, trans. Curt Leviant (New York: Bobbs-Merrill, 1974).

19. See Miron's detailed discussion of Mendele as a character in the fifth chapter of *A Traveler Disguised*.

20. Stillman omits the last sentence in his translation.

21. *Ale Verk* (1928), 2, 8. My translation.

22. This fact, incidentally, may make us question the veracity of the story told at the beginning of this chapter about the history of *Dos Kleyne Mentshele*.

23. Miron, *A Traveler Disguised*, p. 164.

24. Stuart Miller, *The Picaresque Novel* (Cleveland: Case Western Reserve University Press, 1967), p. 72.

25. Samuel Niger, "Yiddish Literature in the Past Two Hundred Years," in *The Jewish People: Past and Present* (New York: CYCO, 1952), 3, 172.

Chapter Four

1. Nachman Maysl, ed., *Dos Mendele Buch* (New York: Yiddisher Kultur Farband, 1959), p. 483.

2. John Dryden, "A Discourse Concerning the Origin and Progress of Satire," in *Essays of John Dryden*, ed., W. P. Ker (New York: Russell and Russell, 1961), 2, 93.

3. All quotations are from *Di Takse*, in *Ale Verk* vol. 4. Unless otherwise noted, all translations are my own.

4. Niger, p. 181.

5. Miron, *A Traveler Disguised*, pp. 141–42.

6. The translation is from *Ibid.*, p. 141.

7. *Ibid.*, p. 143.

8. David Patterson, *The Hebrew Novel in Czarist Russia* (Edinburgh: University of Edinburgh Press, 1964), pp. 12–13.

9. Miron, *A Traveler Disguised*, p. 141.

10. Samuel Niger, *Mendele Mocher Seforim–Zayn lebn, zayn gezelshaftlekhe un literarishe oyftungen*, 2nd rev. ed. (New York: Congress for Jewish Culture, 1970), p. 94.

11. *Ibid.*, pp. 101–102.

12. Other works that have been cited as having influenced the writing of *Di Klyatshe* are Apuleius' *Golden Ass*, Ovid's *Metamorphoses*, and the biblical story of Balaam's ass; but the influence of these works is largely restricted to the ideas of human beings taking on the forms of animals and of animals being able to speak human languages.

13. Sholem Aleichem, p. 34.

14. Niger, "Yiddish Literature," p. 183.

15. Baron, p. 48.

16. *Mendele un zayn Tzeit: Materiale tsu der geshikte fun der yidisher literatur in 19 yahrhundert* (Moscow: Truth Press, 1940), p. 10.

17. Unless otherwise noted, all references are to *The Nag*, trans. Moshe Spiegel (New York: Beechhurst Press, 1955).

18. *Mendele un zayn tzeit*, p. 7.

19. Jacob S. Raisin, *The Haskalah Movement in Russia* (Philadelphia: Jewish Publication Society, 1913), p. 237.

20. *Ibid.*, p. 172.

21. *Encyclopaedia Judaica* (Jerusalem: Keter Publishing House, 1972), III, 754–55. The Hebrew name for Asmodeus is Ashmedai.

22. For the full story see Talmud, Tractate Gittin, 68a–68b.

23. A better translation than "ingenuity" would be "guilelessness."

24. *Kol Kitvey*, p. 318.

Chapter Five

1. Niger, "Yiddish Literature," p. 183.

2. Niger, *Mendele Mocher Seforim*, p. 159. My translation.

3. Paulson, *Satire and the Novel*, p. 33.

4. Paulson, *The Fictions of Satire*, p. 100.

5. Unless otherwise noted, all quotations are from *The Travels and Adventures of Benjamin the Third*, trans. Moshe Spiegel (New York: Schocken Books, 1949).

6. Ruth Wisse, *The Schlemiel as Modern Hero* (Chicago: University of Chicago Press, 1971). When he translated the novel into Hebrew, Abramovitsh added a short epilogue announcing that Benjamin would be leading a tour to Palestine, but this epilogue in no way blunts the abruptness of the book's conclusion.

7. *Ibid.*, pp. 25–40.

8. Wisse believes that their illusions of power are their only recourse in the face of their real powerlessness (*Ibid.*, pp. 35–36). There is certainly merit in this idea, though it is hard to believe that Abramovitsh would condone such a surrender to paralysis.

9. *Dos Mendele Buch*, p. 429. According to Niger (*Mendele Mocher Seforim*, p. 185), Abramovitsh referred to Ahad Ha'am's "Sons of Moses" as "the Red Jews."

10. *Ale Verk* (1928), 9, 69–70. My translation.

11. *Ibid.*, p. 85.

12. *Dos Mendele Buch*, p. 429.

13. *Ibid.*, p. 429.

14. Paulson, *Fictions of Satire*, p. 100.

15. Northrop Frye, *Anatomy of Criticism: Four Essays* (Princeton: Princeton University Press, 1957), p. 228.

16. For an extraordinary description of the problem of the *agunah* see Chaim Grade's novel *The Agunah*.

17. Wisse, pp. 38–39.

Chapter Six

1. *Dos Mendele Buch*, p. 185.

2. *Ibid.*, p. 110, quoted by Miron, *A Traveler Disguised*, p. 107.

3. *Ale Verk* (1928), 10, 6. My translation.

4. Significantly, it is never mentioned in Miron's *A Traveler Disguised*. Miron does make the point that Abramovitsh found Mendele to be almost indispensable in his work (p. 239).

5. *Ale Verk fun Mendele Mocher Seforim* (Warsaw: Farlag Mendele, 1911–1913), vol. XII. This is my only reference to this edition.

6. Viner, p. 46.

7. Unless otherwise noted, all quotations are from *Fishke the Lame*, trans. Gerald Stillman (New York: Thomas Yoseloff, 1960).

8. It used to be a superstitious custom that when a cholera epidemic struck, various cripples and beggars would be married in a cemetery in order to frighten away the disease. I. J. Singer's *Yoshe Kalb* gives a good description of this practice.

9. As Miron shows (*A Traveler Disguised*, pp. 206–12), Abramovitsh's career is a miniature history of the development of the novel in Western Europe.

10. *Ale Verk* (1928), 3, 14. My translation.

11. *Benjamin the Third*, p. 90.

12. For documentation on this point, see Malcolm Hay, *Europe and the Jews: The Pressure of Christendom on the People of Israel for 1900 Years* (Boston: Beacon Press, 1960).

13. Abramovitsh, of course, prepared us for the final discovery when, early in the novel, he had Mendele questioning Alter about his reasons for divorcing his first wife and about their children.

14. Joseph Heller, *Catch-22* (New York: Random House, 1966), p. 427.

15. Isaac Bashevis Singer and Irving Howe, "Yiddish Tradition vs. Jewish Tradition: A Dialogue," *Midstream*, 19 (June–July 1973), 34.

16. See Miron's introduction to *Learn to Do Well*.

17. I. L. Peretz, "Bontsha the Silent," trans. Hilde Abel in *A Treasury of Yiddish Stories*, ed. Irving Howe and Eliezer Greenberg (New York: Viking Press, 1953), p. 230.

18. Miron, introduction to *Learn to Do Well*, p. 49.

19. Isaiah Rabinovich, *Major Trends in Modern Hebrew Fiction*, trans. M. Roston (Chicago: University of Chicago Press, 1968), p. 10.

20. Miron, *A Traveler Disguised*, p. 298, n. 41.

21. Christianity also interpreted the book allegorically, seeing it as describing the relationship between Christ and the Church.

22. Philip Birnbaum, *A Book of Jewish Concepts* (New York: Hebrew Publishing Co., 1964), p. 83.

23. See, for instance, *A Traveler Disguised*, p. 237; and the introduction to *Learn to Do Well*, appendix 4, pp. 116–27.

24. Raisin, pp. 194–95.

25. Miron, *A Traveler Disguised*, p. 92.

26. *Ibid.*, pp. 92–93. This aspect of Abramovitsh's use of Mendele is central to Miron's argument, which is presented here in a somewhat simplified form.

27. Joshua Rothenberg, "Yiddish Literature and Jewish History," *Yiddish* 2 (1975), 2–3.

Chapter Seven

1. *Dos Mendele Buch*, p. 151.
2. *Ibid.*, p. 151.
3. This transformation is the subject of a most important discussion in *A Traveler Disguised*, pp. 95–135.
4. *Ale Verk* (1928), 12, 426, quoted in *A Traveler Disguised*, p. 104.
5. Miron, *A Traveler Disguised*, p. 104.
6. *Ibid.*, pp. 125ff.
7. All quotations are from *Ale Verk* (1928), 11 and 12. My translations.
8. Miron, *A Traveler Disguised*, p. 124.
9. See *Ibid.*, p. 232.
10. It is possible that the valley of Bacha was the name of a particular place that was named for the bacha, the weeping willow, which grew there.
11. *Daily Prayer Book*, trans. and ed. Philip Birnbaum (New York, 1949), p. 246.
12. "Shem and Japhet in the Train," trans. Walter Lever, in *Israel Argosy*, 2 (Spring, 1953), 32.
13. All quotations from the short stories are from *Kol Kitvey*. My translations.

Chapter Eight

1. All quotations are from *Of Bygone Days*, trans. Raymond Sheindlin, in *A Shtetl and Other Yiddish Novellas*, ed. Ruth R. Wisse (New York: Behrman House, 1973).
2. Rothenberg, p. 1.
3. M. Zborowski and E. Herzog, *Life Is with People: The Jewish Little-Town of Eastern Europe* (New York: International Universities Press, 1952), p. 23.

Selected Bibliography

PRIMARY SOURCES

Ale Verk fun Mendele Mocher Seforim. 17 vols. Warsaw: Farlag Mendele, 1911–1913.

Ale Verk fun Mendele Mocher Seforim. 22 vols. ed. N. Maysl. Warsaw: Farlag Mendele, 1928.

Learn to Do Well. ed. Dan Miron. New York: YIVO Institute for Jewish Research, 1969.

Kol Kitvey Mendele Mocher Seforim. Tel Aviv: Hotsa'at Dvir, 1947.

The Parasite. Trans. Gerald Stillman. New York: Thomas Yoseloff, 1956.

The Nag. Trans. Moshe Spiegel. New York: Beechhurst Press, 1955.

The Travels and Adventures of Benjamin the Third. Trans. Moshe Spiegel. New York: Shocken Books, 1949.

Fishke the Lame. Trans. Gerald Stillman. New York: Thomas Yoseloff, 1960.

Of Bygone Days. Trans. Raymond Sheindlin. In *A Shtetl and Other Yiddish Novellas*, ed. Ruth R. Wisse. New York: Behrman House, 1973. Professor Wisse's introduction to this volume is highly recommended.

"The Calf." Trans. Jacob Sloan. in *A Treasury of Yiddish Stories*, ed. I. Howe and E. Greenberg, pp. 97–111. New York: Viking Press, 1954. The introduction to this volume is also very helpful.

"Shem and Japhet in the Train." Trans. Walter Lever. *Israel Argosy*, 2 (Spring 1953), 7–32.

SECONDARY SOURCES

A. Cultural Background

This bibliography includes only some of the more important works on Abramovitsh and his background in English. A more complete bibliography can be found at the end of Miron's *A Traveler Disguised*.

BARON, SALO W. *The Russian Jew Under Tsars and Soviets*. New York: Macmillan, 1964. Excellent survey of cultural and historical conditions in Russia during Abramovitsh's lifetime.

BENJAMIN OF TUDELA. "The Travels of Rabbi Benjamin of Tudela." In *Contemporaries of Marco Polo*, ed. Manuel Komroff. New York: Boni and Liveright, 1928. The story of Benjamin the First, who had such an influence on Benjamin of Tuneyadevka.

BIRNBAUM, PHILIP. *A Book of Jewish Concepts.* New York: Hebrew Publishing Co., 1964. Reference work that defines and describes Jewish religious practices and beliefs.

DAWIDOWICZ, LUCY, ED. *The Golden Tradition—Jewish Life and Thought in Eastern Europe.* New York: Holt, Rinehart, and Winston, 1967. Anthology of contemporaneous essays describing various facets of life in Eastern Europe. The introduction is quite informative.

DUBNOW, SIMON. *History of the Jews.* 10 vols. Trans. Moshe Spiegel. New York: A. S. Barnes and Co., 1971. Interesting description and interpretation of Jewish history by one of Abramovitsh's acquaintances.

Encyclopaedia Judaica. Jerusalem: Keter Publishing House, 1972. Invaluable storehouse of information on Jewish history, culture, and religion.

HESCHEL, ABRAHAM JOSHUA. *The Earth Is the Lord's and The Sabbath.* Philadelphia: Jewish Publication Society, 1962. The first half of this work is a sensitive and beautiful account of Jewish life in Eastern Europe.

MIRON, DAN. *A Traveler Disguised: A Study in the Rise of Modern Yiddish Fiction in the Nineteenth Century.* New York: Schocken Books, 1973. One of the best works ever written about Yiddish literature. Describes the rise of Yiddish literature, but concentrates on Abramovitsh's works, especially the prefaces.

ZBOROWSKI, M. AND E. HERZOG. *Life Is with People: The Jewish Little-Town of Eastern Europe.* New York: International Universities Press, 1952. Sociological study of the *shtetl.*

B. General Studies

The following articles and books provide interesting surveys of the development of Yiddish and Hebrew literature.

LIPTZIN, SOL. *The Flowering of Yiddish Literature.* New York: Thomas Yoseloff, 1963.

————. *A History of Yiddish Literature.* New York: Jonathan David Publishers, 1972.

MADISON, CHARLES A. *Yiddish Literature: Its Scope and Major Writers.* New York: Frederick Ungar, 1968.

NIGER, SAMUEL. "Yiddish Literature in the Past Two Hundred Years." In *The Jewish People: Past and Present,* III, 165–218. New York: CYCO, 1952.

ROBACK, A. A. *The Story of Yiddish Literature.* New York: YIVO, 1940.

SILBERSCHLAG, EISIG. *From Renaissance to Renaissance: Hebrew Literature from 1492–1970.* New York: Ktav, 1973. Vol. I.

WAXMAN, MEYER. "Modern Hebrew Literature." In *The Jewish People: Past and Present*, III, 103–44. New York: CYCO, 1952.
WIENER, LEO. *The History of Yiddish Literature in the Nineteenth Century.* New York: Scribner's, 1899.

Index

(The works of Abramovitsh are listed in both Yiddish and Hebrew under his name.)

172